Rosemary Haughton
Witness to Hope

Eilish Ryan

Sheed & Ward

Kansas City

Grateful acknowledgment is given to the following publishers for permission to use extended quotations from copyrighted works.

Material taken from *The Theology of Experience* by Rosemary Haughton published and copyright © 1972 by Darton, Longman and Todd Ltd and used by permission of the publishers. Material from *The Passionate God* by Rosemary Haughton published and copyright © 1981 by Darton, Longman and Todd Ltd and used by permission of the publishers.

On Trying to Be Human by Rosemary Haughton, copyright © 1966; *The Re-Creation of Eve* by Rosemary Haughton, copyright © 1985; and *Song in a Strange Land* by Rosemary Haughton, copyright © 1990. Reprinted by permission of Templegate Publishers, Springfield, IL.

Sheed & Ward™ is a service of National Catholic Reporter Publishing Company, Inc.

Library of Congress Cataloging-in-Publication Data:
Ryan, Eilish, 1943-
    Rosemary Haughton : witness to hope / Eilish
Ryan.
        p. cm.
    Includes bibliographical references.
    ISBN: 1-55612-860-6 (alk. paper)
     1. Haughton, Rosemary. I. Title.
BX4705.H3335R93 1997
282'.092—dc21   97-20332
   [B]   CIP

Published by: Sheed & Ward
                115 E. Armour Blvd., P.O. Box 419492
                Kansas City, MO 64141-6492.

To order, call: (800)333-7373

www.natcath.com/sheedward

Cover photograph of Rosemary Haughton by Thomas Merton.

Cover designed by Jane Pitz.

Contents

Dedicated to
my mother and grandmothers,
all women of faith and hope
in their own times

Frances Vera Woods Ryan
Susan Butler Woods
Elizabeth Ryan Ryan

ACKNOWLEDGMENTS

I am indebted to many people whose insights and encouragement have contributed to the evolution of this book about the life and writings of Rosemary Haughton as a witness to the power of Christian hope. For their support and scholarly critique during the doctoral studies phase, I am particularly grateful to Professors Ellen Leonard, Lorna Bowman, Margaret Brennan, Annice Callahan and Steve Dunn at the Toronto School of Theology, Toronto, Ontario, Canada. I am also very grateful to the late Professor Walter Principe of the Pontifical Institute for Mediaeval Studies, Toronto, for his wise advice, to Professor Frank Fletcher, St. Paul's Seminary, Sydney, Australia, for his comments on Chapter Three, and to Professor Michael Downey, Gonzaga University, Spokane, Washington, for his careful reading of a preliminary draft and for his encouragement in seeking publication.

For their assistance and patience in the publication phase, I am grateful to Andy Apathy and Sarah Smiley at Sheed & Ward. I also acknowledge with gratitude colleagues at the University of the Incarnate Word, San Antonio, Texas, who graciously made time to read and comment on chapters of the manuscript.

My thanks also go to the Congregation of the Sisters of Charity of the Incarnate Word of San Antonio, Texas, who generously supported me during my doctoral studies. I am especially grateful to those whose belief in me kept me going when my self-confidence wavered and my energy waned.

Last, but certainly not least, I express my appreciation to Rosemary Haughton for her encouragement during the entire project, for her generous assistance with the biographical material, and also for the inspiration of her example and hospitality during my week-long stay at Wellspring House in February, 1993.

Eilish Ryan, C.C.V.I.
January 19, 1997

Introduction

Our experience of God and our spirituality must emerge from our concrete, historical situation and must return to that situation to feed and enliven it. . . . Our time and place in history bring us face to face with profound societal impasse. Here God makes demands for conversion, healing, justice, love, compassion, solidarity, and communion. Here the face of God appears, a God who dies in human beings and rises in human freedom and dignity.

 – Constance FitzGerald, "Impasse and Dark Night"[1]

A century ago, people awaited the twentieth century with hope and expectation. They hoped that the next hundred years would see the eradication of communicable diseases, poverty, and hunger. They expected the advancement of all levels of society through the constructive use of energy and science and the cessation of war. At the approach of the new century, many established citizens of the Western world perceived themselves to be living in the best and most hopeful of eras, characterized by a burgeoning economy and improvements in public health, science, and technology. Beneath the apparent tranquility and prosperity, however, a new cultural revolution was already brewing as

---

1. Constance FitzGerald, O.C.D., "Impasse and Dark Night," in *Women's Spirituality*, ed. Joann Wolski Conn (Mahwah, NJ: Paulist Press, 1986), 288, 299.

ix

early as the 1880s as the superficial culture began to lose its underpinnings.

Early in the twentieth century, the inherent weaknesses of the period asserted themselves and ultimately resulted in two world wars, major economic depression, international tension, the Cold War, and a global environmental crisis. As the twentieth century draws to a close, it is clear that it did not see the end of human suffering. We still face situations of war, disease, political upheaval, schism, and apocalypticism, in ever more frightening guises.

Futurist Alvin Toffler points out that, in addition to the crises themselves, modern culture impacts people with accelerated change and a consequent sense of impermanence, transience, and a crisis of limits.[2] David Griffin characterizes the complex social phenomenon of modernity in terms of dichotomization, differentiation, mechanization, and materialism.[3] Through his social analysis, Joe Holland identifies the machine as the root metaphor for the modern age. It is no wonder that pastoral theologian Henri Nouwen speaks of the prevailing backdrop of fear at this time: "Most of us people of the twentieth century live in the house of fear most of the time. It has become an obvious dwelling place, an acceptable basis on which to make our decisions and plan our lives."[4]

It is evident that the marvels of technology have neither gifted us with a new level of consciousness nor protected

---

2. Alvin Toffler's analyses of current and future trends are found in *Future Shock* (New York: Bantam Books, 1970), *The Third Wave* (New York: Bantam Books, 1980), *Powershift: Knowledge, Wealth, and Violence at the Edge of the 21st Century* (New York: Bantam Books, 1990).

3. David R. Griffin, "Introduction: Postmodern Spirituality and Society," in *Spirituality and Society: Postmodern Visions*, ed. D.R. Griffin (New York: SUNY, 1988), 1-31.

4. Henri J. M. Nouwen, *Lifesigns* (New York: Doubleday, 1989), 15.

us from our own less sophisticated responses. Despite our scientific achievements, we stand before the great questions of life, in ever larger dimensions, with little more inner resources than our ancestors.

In reflecting on this situation in her essay "Impasse and Dark Night," American Carmelite Constance FitzGerald suggests that there is not only a dark night of the soul, but also a dark night of the world, a societal experience of impasse in which every logical attempt to resolve world problems fails. She also perceives a similarity between the characteristics of the individual spiritual dark night, described so profoundly by John of the Cross, and aspects of the global situation today.

In a genuine experience of the spiritual dark night, the person finds no joy where previously there had been joy. Hope, faith, and the capacity for prayer are elusive. Every attempt to regain the former state of consolation comes to nothing, only further darkness. The dark night is an experience of human limitation that exposes humankind's fragility, brokenness, dependence, and lack of integration.

FitzGerald uses the term *impasse* to refer to a situation in which "there is no way out, no way around, no rational escape from what imprisons one, no possibilities in the situation."[5] In a true impasse, not only is ordinary activity frustrated, but also every rationally attempted solution fails. Despair becomes a real temptation in the face of seeming hopelessness, disappointment, and loss of meaning. Addressing contemporary experience, FitzGerald poses the challenging and even disturbing question: "What if, by chance, our time in evolution is a dark-night time – a time of crisis and transition that must be understood if it is to be part of learning a new vision and harmony for the human species and the planet?"[6]

5. FitzGerald, 288.
6. Ibid.

Confronted with this possibility, FitzGerald believes that it is precisely the seemingly overwhelmed imagination that is needed to enter more deeply into the situation. Paradoxically, the situation that seems to have no potential is, in reality, the very situation through which new life can emerge. Like Dorothée Soelle, FitzGerald believes that the release of the imaginative forces capable of breaking through impasse or the dark night requires letting go of the conceptual blocks that often limit our thinking. In a situation of genuine impasse, change can only occur through a creative response arising from a new inner vision.[7]

At the same time, FitzGerald stresses that any truly Christian response to the issues of today must be grounded in the concrete, historical situation because it is the place where we meet God:

> Our time and place in history bring us face to face with profound societal impasse. Here God makes demands for conversion, healing, justice, love, compassion, solidarity, and communion. Here the face of God appears, a God who dies in human beings and rises in human freedom and dignity.[8]

FitzGerald also believes that the experience of impasse can be the condition for creative growth and change only if the experience and the human condition itself are faced honestly in a spirit of surrender to the mystery of life. In reference to societal impasse, she writes:

> It is only in the process of bringing the impasse to prayer, to the perspective of the God who loves us, that our society will be freed, healed, changed, brought to paradoxical new vision, and freed for nonviolent,

---

7. Ibid., 290.
8. Ibid., 299.

selfless, liberating action, freed, therefore, for community on this planet earth.[9]

Such radically honest, faithfilled, and creative revisioning, however, is alien to a culture that relies on the judgment of hard logic and the power of technology to resolve its problems. Nevertheless, alternative visions and new spiritualities are emerging in this period of darkness. Individuals and groups in whom hope has not died invite the world once again to the possibility of new life in the mystery of the peace and justice of God.

In this book, I propose that Rosemary Haughton is one of the people in whom hope has not died. In her lifetime she has faced the darkness of this time radically, both from the depths of her own experience and from her careful analysis of her Christian faith and pressing contemporary issues. She models an imaginative, compassionate, and hope-filled response to the contemporary experience of impasse. Through her writings and example she is a resource for people who are seeking a creative and positive approach to the challenges which face humanity as we enter the twenty-first century.

The earliest seeds of this book were my own experiences and questions. During my doctoral studies at the Toronto School of Theology, I had the opportunity to sort and clarify my ideas. I began the doctoral program with a desire to study in the area of pastoral theology in order to explore how the Christian tradition could better speak to the contemporary world, particularly on the personal level.[10]

---

9. Ibid., 301.

10. Robert L. Kinast, in "How Pastoral Theology Functions," *Theology Today* 37 (Jan. 1981): 425, writes: "The task of facilitating the interaction between academic theology and pastoral ministry belongs in a preeminent way to pastoral theology." Karl Rahner, in "Practical Theology within the Totality of Theological Disciplines," in *Theological Investigations*, vol. 9, trans. Graham Harrison (New York: Herder and Herder, 1972), 102, states that pastoral theology is concerned with

In particular, I wanted to investigate how the Christian message could support and encourage people today as they struggle with their own lives and the broader societal issues of our time.

This determination grew out of my experience teaching various secondary- and university-level religious studies courses and working with campus ministry, adult religious education, and retreat programs. In each of these settings, which were primarily within the Roman Catholic tradition, I encountered sincere people who recognized a painful gap between their vision of the Christian ideal and the seeming irrelevance of faith in their everyday lives. Their stories touched me. Their struggles convinced me of the need for more role models to enable Catholics and other Christians to develop an internalized faith vision and a mature spirituality through which they could relate their faith to their deepest hopes and their daily experiences. Despite my own questions and struggles, I believed that the Christian tradition, revitalized for many Roman Catholics by the Second Vatican Council (1962-1965), held the wisdom for a new approach to spirituality.

During my studies, I discovered the breadth of the emerging field of Christian spirituality. I became more aware of the cultural shifts which have defined the twentieth century and to which contemporary theology has attempted to respond. I also became increasingly conscious of the feminist issues involved in theology and the church today. Gradually, my interests turned toward contemporary approaches to Christian spirituality through which women and men could integrate their faith with their everyday experience and participate in the effort toward peace and justice

---

the self-actualization of the Church through theological illumination of the situation in which it finds itself and in relation to which it must develop.

in the human community. When I was introduced to Haughton's work, I immediately recognized that her story and writings provided a basis through which I could explore these topics.

Rosemary Haughton (1927-), a twentieth-century British and American Roman Catholic author, lecturer, and social advocate, has maintained a lifelong avid interest in philosophical and theological questions. She has been actively involved in social issues and alternative lifestyle Christian communities. As a wife and the mother of ten children and four foster children, she has combined very demanding family obligations with an almost restless investigation of the meaning of Catholicism and mature Christian consciousness today. Familiar with the ordinary stuff of life, teething babies, preparations for school plays, hospitalized children, family and financial crises, and elderly parents, Haughton applies her understanding of the gospel to life as she experiences it in her family, culture, work and church. As a lay Roman Catholic, she contributes to and exemplifies in a special way the development of the laity envisioned by the Second Vatican Council.[11]

Haughton's published works include over two hundred articles, numerous pamphlets, twenty-eight books for children, and thirty books on religious and theological topics related to the meaning of Christian faith and experience in today's world. Her major works include *On Trying to Be Human* (1966), a reflection on the meaning of human life; *The Transformation of Man* (1967), a study of conversion

---

11. The role of the laity is addressed in many of the documents of the Second Vatican Council. See in particular "The Laity," *Lumen Gentium* Ch. 4, no. 30-38, pp. 56-65, and "The Call of the Whole Church to Holiness," Ch. 5, no. 39-42, pp. 65-72 in Walter M. Abbott, S.J. ed., *The Documents of Vatican II* (New York: The America Press, 1966). See also the same council's document on the laity *Apostolicam Actuositatem*, ibid., 489-521.

and community; *The Passionate God* (1981), a response to her own question, "What difference does the Resurrection make?" and *The Re-Creation of Eve* (1985), a feminist reconstruction of a number of Gospel passages on the empowering relationship of Jesus with women. In *Song in a Strange Land* (1990) she recounts the vision and work of Wellspring House, where she has worked with homeless women and children since 1981. In her most recent book, *Images for Change* (1997), she points out how the breakdown of structures of meaning in society provides an opportunity to rebuild a better world.

Although Haughton's formal education extended only through high school and some post-secondary art courses, her writing has been widely recognized by both the academic community and a general religious audience in the United States, Britain, Ireland, Canada, and Australia. Several colleges and universities have awarded her honorary doctoral degrees in theology or letters.[12] Her creative insights into the dynamics of contemporary Christian life have been cited by numerous authors.[13]

---

12. The honorary degrees Haughton has received include a Doctor of Letters for her writing (Nazareth College, Rochester, 1975), a Doctor of Divinity for her theological insight (St. Mary's College, Notre Dame, 1976), a Doctor of Humane Letters for her efforts in the area of human relationships (Georgian Court College, Lakewood, New Jersey, 1983). The University of Dayton awarded Haughton its 1987 Marianist Award for her contributions, by both word and example, to the renewal of the church. She has presented papers at numerous conferences and scholarly conventions, including the Catholic Theological Society of America.

13. Among others, Denise Lardner Carmody, "A Vision," in *Seizing the Apple* (New York: Crossroad, 1984), 13-31, draws on Haughton's sense of Divine Wisdom and the passionate fire of love underlying Christianity; in her *Virtuous Woman: Reflections on Christian Feminist Ethics* (Maryknoll: Orbis, 1992) Carmody cites Haughton as an example of commitment to the feminine vision of Jesus (37-43) and of feminist ethics (166-67). Walter E. Conn, "Affective Conversion: The

Despite the fact that Haughton's work has been widely read and acclaimed, no systematic study has been undertaken. This book provides the first biography of Haughton, an analysis of her theology and spirituality, and a comprehensive bibliography of her writings in religion and theology for adults. It is my hope that this work will encourage future studies into various dimensions of Haughton's thought and action.

Since both the meaning of the term *spirituality* and the academic discipline engaged in the study of Christian spirituality are subjects of ongoing discussion, Chapter One provides a frame of reference for the other chapters through a survey of current thought on the study of Christian spirituality. Chapter Two presents a biographical sketch of Rosemary Haughton because, as Sandra Schneiders points out in her essay "Spirituality in the Academy," spirituality is primarily a personal experience that cannot be studied in theoretical isolation from the cultural, historical, and religious contexts of the individual.[14] This biographical sketch also identifies many of the theological, literary, and other resources from which Haughton draws her images and concepts.

Transformation of Desire," in *Religion and Culture*, ed. T. P. Fallon, S.J. and P. B. Riley (New York: SUNY, 1987), 266-70, in his discussion of B. Lonergan's concept of affective conversion as transformation of desire, incorporates Haughton's concepts of romantic and personal transformation. Elizabeth Dreyer, *Manifestations of Grace* (Wilmington: Michael Glazier, 1990), 192, cites Haughton's discussion in *The Theology of Experience* about the importance of the church recognizing its position in and not apart from the world. Matthew Lamb, *Solidarity with Victims* (New York: Crossroad, 1982), chap. 1 n. 25, refers to her insights on the relationship between agapic love and work for justice.

14. Sandra Schneiders, "Spirituality in the Academy," *Theological Studies* 50 (1989): 692-95.

Since the definition of Christian spirituality used here indicates that a Christian understanding of humanity's ultimate concern is integral to a Christian spirituality, Chapter Three explores Haughton's theology. It includes her methodology and Christian anthropology, and her presentation of important theological concepts.

Chapter Four focuses specifically on Haughton's expression of a contemporary Christian spirituality through an examination of her approach to significant issues in Christian spirituality. It addresses her understanding of spirituality, holiness, conversion, and spiritual growth; her image of personal and societal transformation as the goal of Christian spirituality; and the role of social concern in her spirituality, particularly her emphasis on the relationship between prayer and politics, between Christian faith and ecology, and between feminist concerns and the role of the church in facilitating such transformation.[15]

---

15. In developing this approach to the study of Rosemary Haughton's spirituality, I am indebted to the suggestions made by Joann Wolski Conn in her essay "Horizons on Contemporary Spirituality," *Horizons* 9 (1982): 60-73. Although I have followed inclusive-language usage, I have kept direct quotations in the original form to allow a sense of Haughton's and other authors' development in the use of inclusive language. Also, quotations from Haughton's works appear in the original British or American English.

Chapter One

Contemporary Christian Spirituality

The word spirituality *comes from "spirit," which is biblical language for life, force, or energy. It is the opposite of emptiness, of what is destructive, of death. In a different sense, it is the opposite of pure theory. To be spiritual is not to "know" but to "live."*
— Néstor Jaén, *Toward a Liberation Spirituality*[1]

Christian spirituality is a vast topic that can be investigated from a variety of perspectives. Because the word *spirituality* itself is a fluid and elusive term, its usage requires clarification in any discussion. For this reason, although this book focuses on Rosemary Haughton and her expression of a hope-filled spirituality that responds to the realities of today's world, it is important at the outset to take some time to establish a frame of reference for the chapters that follow.

The first section describes the relatively recent phenomenon of a widespread surge of interest in spirituality. The second section summarizes the history of the word *spirituality* and describes its use in the present context. Lastly, the third section briefly addresses contemporary approaches to the academic study of Christian spirituality. This discussion focuses primarily, although not exclusively, on

---

1. Néstor Jaén, S.J., *Toward a Liberation Spirituality* (Chicago: Loyola University Press, 1991), 3.

Christian spirituality in the United States, particularly since the Second Vatican Council.

Renewed Interest in Spirituality

We encounter the word *spirituality* so frequently and in such diverse settings today that it is hard to realize that this extensive and varied use of the term is a recent phenomenon. Since the late 1960s, a significant change has occurred not only in the frequency of its use but also in the commonly understood meaning of the term. Less than half a century ago, spirituality referred principally to a narrow, privatized, and primarily Roman Catholic focus on "the interior life." Today, spirituality encompasses an experiential and holistic concept of the Christian life which is discussed across denominational boundaries. Protestants, previously suspicious of the term because of its connection with religious enthusiasm and mysticism, now not only use the word with its Catholic meanings but also incorporate insights from their own traditions.

A renewed interest in spirituality as lived Christian experience is evident on the popular level in the proliferation of articles and books about Christian spirituality and in the development of countless workshops, seminars, courses, and retreats on the topic. This growing interest in Christian spirituality among both Catholics and other Christians since the late 1960s has been well documented and studied by scholars, cultural commentators, and the press.[2]

---

2. John L. Elias, "The Return of Spirituality: Contrasting Interpretations," *Religious Education* 86 (Summer 1991): 455-65, examines general cultural and societal factors involved in the revival of spirituality in the United States. James Bacik, in his article "Contemporary Spirituality" in the *New Dictionary of Catholic Spirituality* (Collegeville: Liturgical Press, 1993), 214-20, examines the findings of several surveys

In its broadest current usage, the word *spirituality* is no longer limited to Christianity or even to the realm of religion. For example, in his discussion of the cultural shift from modern to post-modern society, David Ray Griffin uses the term *spirituality* in the sense of "the ultimate values and meanings in terms of which we live, whether they be otherworldly or very worldly ones, and whether or not we consciously try to increase our commitment to those values and meanings."[3]

On the academic level, scholars have addressed both the meaning of spirituality and the discipline that studies it.[4] Courses and programs on spirituality at the university level have multiplied. Critical editions of many major texts on spirituality in Christianity and other world religions are now available in English. Specialized dictionaries and other resources for scholars in the area of spirituality continue to

related to changes in Roman Catholic spirituality in the U.S. since the Second Vatican Council.

3. Griffin, "Introduction: Postmodern Spirituality and Society," 1.

4. For a thorough discussion of the term *spirituality*, developments in the academic study of spirituality, and the relationship between spirituality and theology, see Walter Principe, "Toward Defining Spirituality," *Studies in Religion/Sciences religieuses* 12 (Spring 1983): 127-41. A condensed and revised version of this article may be found under "Spirituality, Christian," in the *New Dictionary of Christian Spirituality*, 931-38. The scholarly multi-volume *Dictionnaire de spiritualité ascétique et mystique doctrine et histoire*, vol. 14 (Paris: Beauchesne, 1990), under "Spiritualité," cols. 1142-73, comments on the issues at length. In addition to resources already mentioned, other good sources include Sandra Schneiders, "Theology and Spirituality: Strangers, Rivals, or Partners?" *Horizons* 13 (1986): 253-74; Michael Downey, "Understanding Christian Spirituality: Dress Rehearsal for a Method," *Spirituality Today* 43 (Fall 1991): 271-80; and Joann Wolski Conn's essay "Spirituality" in *The New Dictionary of Theology*, Joseph A. Komonchak, Mary Collins, Dermot Lane, eds. (Wilmington, Del.: Michael Glazier, 1987), 972-86; Lawrence S. Cunningham and Keith J. Egan, *Christian Spirituality: Themes from the Tradition* (Mahwah, NJ: Paulist Press, 1996).

be published.[5] The Society for the Study of Christian Spirituality, which was established in 1992, promotes research and dialogue within the growing interdisciplinary field of spirituality.

This noticeable increase of interest in Christian spirituality over the last three decades did not originate in the classroom, however. It sprang from cultural changes in the post-World War II period and especially from the intensified religious experience of Christians, mostly Roman Catholics, following the Second Vatican Council. In the wake of the ferment of the sixties, interest in spirituality flourished through the influence of spiritual teachers from the Orient and the rise of existential, humanistic, and transpersonal psychologies. Changing patterns of American social life, including suburban expansion, increased education, the civil rights movement, the women's movement, and a growing concern about the environment, prompted a broader interpretation of spirituality. At the same time, world events, including famine, war, and political turmoil, inspired a new global perspective on spirituality.

In addition to these cultural influences, the theological and practical developments generated by the Second Vatican Council had a profound impact on the scriptural, ecclesial, liturgical, and social foundations of contemporary Roman Catholic spirituality. The Council's insistence on the universal

---

5. Particularly of note are the massive Paulist Press project, "Classics of Western Spirituality," which began in 1978; the multi-volume *World Spirituality: An Encyclopedic History of the Religious Quest* series (New York: Crossroad, 1985-) in which Christianity is addressed in vols. 16-18: *Christian Spirituality I: Origins to the Twelfth Century* (1985), eds. B. McGinn and J. Meyendorff, *Christian Spirituality II: High Middle Ages and Reformation* (1987), eds. Jill Raitt, J. Meyendorff, and B. McGinn, *Christian Spirituality III: Post-Reformation and Modern* (1989), eds. Louis Dupré and Don E. Saliers; *The New Dictionary of Catholic Spirituality*; and *The Westminster Dictionary of Christian Spirituality*, ed. Gordon Wakefield (Philadelphia: Westminster, 1983).

call to holiness signaled the need for a contemporary spirituality nourished within the church but active in the broader community.[6] As theologian Anne Patrick suggests, the current popularity of spirituality may be due to the way in which Christian spirituality, in contrast to the ethical and systematic disciplines within theology, has created a space where religious experience is able to interpret and express itself.[7]

Although this marked growth of interest in spirituality may seem random in many respects, Sandra Schneiders identifies four general patterns in the various developments in Christian spirituality during the post-conciliar period.[8] In the first approach, spirituality is equated principally with an individual's personal prayer life. Those who favor this approach frequently participate in the charismatic renewal, private retreats, and other personal prayer experiences.

In the second approach, which incorporates a slightly wider understanding of spirituality, spirituality is related not only with prayer but also with an intense, faith-filled engagement in daily activities. The Cursillo movement, Marriage Encounter and other programs that provide intense, short-term faith experiences as a foundation for a deeper Christian life represent this approach. Ongoing spiritual direction, faith-sharing groups, and study groups are often expressions of this understanding of spirituality as well.

---

6. See *Lumen Gentium*, chap. 5., especially par. 40: "All Christians in any state or walk of life are called to the fullness of Christian life and to the perfection of love."

7. Anne E. Patrick, "Ethics and Spirituality: The Social Justice Connection," *Way Supplement* 63 (Autumn 1988): 107.

8. See Schneiders, "Theology and Spirituality," 253-54. In his essay "Contemporary Spirituality," in the *New Dictionary of Catholic Spirituality*, 215-17, James Bacik provides a chronological analysis of a number of post-conciliar developments in Roman Catholic spirituality.

In addition to personal prayer and an intensified awareness of the faith dimension of daily life, Schneiders mentions
a third and still broader view of spirituality that incorporates
the whole of personal experience, particularly the bodily
and emotional experiences so often discounted or rejected
by earlier Roman Catholic moral and spiritual teaching.
Today, advocates of holistic and bodily spiritualities emphasize the integration of the material dimensions of being
human into a well-developed Christian life.

The fourth post-conciliar approach to spirituality identified by Schneiders stresses the relationship between Christian commitment and social and political life, particularly
with respect to justice and to feminist and ecological issues.
Many proponents of this emphasis in spirituality are actively
engaged in social and political as well as religious advocacy
groups and reform movements.

Schneiders emphasizes that, although these various
approaches to Christian spirituality did not develop in strict
chronological order, there seems to have been a progression
from a focus on personal prayer experience to a wider vision
of spirituality that encompasses the whole of life, including
its societal and global contexts. At the same time, in discussing various approaches to spirituality it is important to
recognize that they are not mutually exclusive. In fact, as
Schneiders notes, all four approaches are usually operative
in varying degrees whenever Christian spirituality is considered today. Furthermore, it is not always clear which approach predominates in a given situation.

In response to what Schneiders calls the spirituality
phenomenon, a number of scholars have sought to sharpen
the contemporary understanding of the term *spirituality* and
the lived reality that it expresses. These studies are complex
because spirituality is not a single, transcultural phenomenon. It is rooted in the lived experience of God's presence
in history, a history that is always particular and specific.[9]

The following section draws on some of these studies to provide a background for the discussion of Rosemary Haughton's spirituality.

Understandings of Christian Spirituality

Walter Principe was among the first to attempt to clarify the contemporary understanding of spirituality. In "Toward Defining Spirituality," he approaches the problem by distinguishing three different but related categories or levels of spirituality.[10] Principe identifies the first and most basic category of spirituality as the real or experiential level, which he describes as "the way in which a person understands and lives within his or her historical context that aspect of his or her religion, philosophy or ethic that is viewed as the loftiest, the noblest, the most calculated to lead to the fullness of the ideal or perfection being sought."[11]

For Principe, specifically Christian spirituality is situated in "life in the Spirit as brothers and sisters in Jesus Christ and daughters and sons of the Father." The experiential level of Christian spirituality, therefore, embraces the whole person, both as an individual and as a member of society, as he or she responds to the call and gifts of the Spirit.

Principe's second category moves from a personal to a group expression of spirituality. This form of spirituality often begins informally within the family and later extends to a parish or other groups. It frequently includes the

---

9. Philip Sheldrake, *Spirituality and History: Questions of Interpretation and Method* (New York: Crossroad, 1992), 33.

10. Principe, "Toward Defining Spirituality," 135-37; see also his article "Spirituality, Christian," in the *New Dictionary of Christian Spirituality*, 932-34. A Basilian priest, Principe was for many years a professor at the Pontifical Institute of Mediaeval Studies in Toronto, Canada.

11. Principe, "Toward Defining Spirituality," 135.

formulation of teachings about the lived experience, often under the influence of some outstanding spiritual leader or in a particular social context. In this sense, various Christian spiritualities have arisen over the centuries, including the Dominican, Carmelite, and Jesuit traditions, as well as the *devotio moderna* and other spiritualities that focus primarily on the interior life for clergy or laity. In addition, Western and Eastern Catholic spiritualities, a number of denominational spiritualities, and the spiritualities of various lay movements have emerged.[12] In the last decades of the twentieth century, increased political and social consciousness has generated liberation, creation-centered, feminist, and ecological emphases in Christian spirituality.[13]

---

12. Annice Callahan, ed., *Spiritualities of the Heart: Approaches to Personal Wholeness in Christian Tradition* (New York: Paulist Press, 1990), through a series of essays by noted authors in spirituality presents a survey of a number of major Christian spiritual writers across the centuries who speak of the mysterious center of the human person in a holistic and experiential way.

13. Representative works include Robert McAfee Brown, *Spirituality and Liberation: Overcoming the Great Fallacy* (Philadelphia: Westminster, 1988); Gustavo Gutiérrez, *We Drink from Our Own Wells: The Spiritual Journey of a People*, trans. Matthew J. O'Connell (Maryknoll: Orbis, 1984); Dorothée Soelle, *The Window of Vulnerability: A Political Spirituality* (Minneapolis: Fortress, 1990); Mathew Fox, *Original Blessing* (Santa Fe: Bear and Company, 1987); Anne Carr, *Transforming Grace: Christian Tradition and Women's Experience* (San Francisco: Harper and Row, 1988); Katherine Zappone, *The Hope for Wholeness: A Spirituality for Feminists* (Mystic, Conn.: Twenty-Third Publications, 1991); Mary Condren, *The Serpent and the Goddess* (New York: Harper, 1989); Ann O'Hara Graff, ed., *In the Embrace of God: Feminist Approaches to Theological Anthropology* (Maryknoll: Orbis, 1995); Jay McDaniel, *Earth, Sky, Gods and Mortals: Developing an Ecological Spirituality* (Mystic, Conn.: Twenty-Third Publications, 1990); Rosemary R. Ruether, *Gaia and God: An Ecofeminist Theology of Earth Healing* (San Francisco: Harper, 1992); Elizabeth Dreyer, *Earth Crammed with Heaven: A Spirituality of Everyday Life* (Mahwah: Paulist Press, 1994); Mary Heather McKinnon and Moni McIntyre, eds., *Readings in Ecological and Feminist Theology* (Kansas City, Mo.: Sheed & Ward, 1995).

The third category of spirituality described by Principe encompasses the formal study of the first and especially of the second levels of spirituality. In this category, spirituality becomes a scholarly discipline using the methods and resources of several branches of knowledge, including theology, religious studies, and the social sciences.

Principe's description of the experiential, devotional, and scholarly levels of spirituality provides a valuable framework for further studies in the field. A starting point in many studies is the examination of the history and use of the word *spirituality* itself. These studies are both interesting and significant because they provide an overview of the development of spirituality in Western Christianity.

History of the Term Spirituality

The modern English word *spirituality* and its linguistic cognates, including *spiritualité, Spiritualität,* and *spiritualità,* have their origin in a fifth-century Latin word, *spiritualitas,* which has a complex history tied to the shifting sense of the reality it designated under various philosophical and historical influences.[14] Jean LeClerq distinguishes two major periods in the evolution of the term *spiritualitas.*[15]

---

14. For a concise and thorough presentation of the history of the term, refer to Principe, "Toward Defining Spirituality," 130-35, in which he summarizes and augments the work of Jean Leclerq in "'Spiritualitas,'" *Studi medievali* 3 (1962): 279-96. Leclerq in turn drew on the earlier full-length work of Lucy Tinsley, *The French Expressions for Spiritualité: A Semantic Study* (Washington, D.C.: Catholic University of America, 1953). See also Principe, "Spirituality, Christian," *New Dictionary of Catholic Spirituality,* 931-32. Sheldrake, *Spirituality and History,* 34-44, suggests additional materials and references. For a comprehensive presentation, see A. Solignac, "Spiritualité: le mot et l'histoire," *Dictionnaire de spiritualité,* vol. 14, cols. 1142-60.

15. Leclerq, "'Spiritualitas,'" 279.

From its origin in the fifth century until the twelfth century, it referred to life under the influence of the Holy Spirit. With the rise of scholasticism in the Middle Ages, *spiritualitas* acquired new and diverse meanings.

The Latin noun *spiritualitas* was coined in ecclesiastical Latin from the noun *spiritus* (spirit) and the adjective *spiritualis* (spiritual), translations in turn of the Greek *pneuma* and *pneumatikos* which appear in the Pauline writings. As Principe emphasizes, it is important to keep in mind that in Pauline theology *pneuma* and *pneumatikos* are not contrasted with *soma* (body) and *somatikos* but with *sarx* (flesh) and *sarkikos*:

> For Paul, the "spirit" within the human person is all that is ordered, led, or influenced by the *Pneuma Theou* or *Spiritus Dei*, whereas *sarx* or *caro* or "flesh" is everything in a person that is opposed to this influence of the Spirit of God. Thus *caro* or "flesh" could be the person's mind or will or heart as much as or even more than the physical flesh or the body if the mind, will, or heart resist the influence of the Spirit.[16]

This sense is evident, for instance, in I Cor. 2:14-15 where the "spiritual person" mentioned is not someone who tries to escape from reality, but rather one in whom the Spirit of God dwells as opposed to the "natural" or "unspiritual" person who disdains the things of God.[17] It is important to note that the contrast here is between two ways of life or attitudes to life rather than between the material and the immaterial dimensions of life. This distinction will be important for understanding Haughton's approach to Christian theology and spirituality.

---

16. Principe, "Toward Defining Spirituality," 130.
17. Schneiders, "Theology and Spirituality," 258.

In the twelfth century, this important distinction gradually faded under the influence of the new philosophy on theology. *Spiritualitas* lost its inclusive Pauline sense and came to designate the non-material in contrast to the material (*materialitas* or *corporalitas*), or the rational as opposed to the non-rational in human experience.[18] This new usage shifted the emphasis from the experience of life in the Spirit to a focus on essence. With reference to this development, Principe remarks that "in this shift one can foresee the confusion of spirituality with disdain for the body and matter that was to mark many later movements dealing with spiritual life."[19]

While the new dualistic interpretation of *spiritualitas* only gradually, and sometimes hesitatingly, gained acceptance, the earlier holistic sense endured for some time. As Principe notes, for instance, "In the majority of Thomas' texts *spiritualitas* is related to the Pauline notion of life according to the Holy Spirit or life according to what is highest in the human person; in a good number of texts, however, it is set in opposition to corporeity or to matter."[20]

A further complication arose during the thirteenth century when a new legal application contrasted *spiritualitas* with *temporalitas* to distinguish ecclesiastical property from the property of the secular ruler. From the thirteenth to the sixteenth century, this juridical usage gradually predominated and the earlier philosophical and theological meanings of *spiritualitas* declined, although they never totally disappeared.

Meanwhile, the Latin *spiritualitas* gave rise to the medieval vernacular forms *espiritualité* in French and spirituality in English. At first, both of these words referred to the

---

18. Sheldrake, *Spirituality and History*, 35.
19. Principe, "Toward Defining Spirituality," 131.
20. Ibid.

religious realm or to ecclesiastical persons or property. Later they developed the philosophical senses often found in medieval Latin.[21]

In the seventeenth century, sometimes called the golden age of Christian spirituality, the religious meaning of *spiritualité* reappeared in Roman Catholic use in France, where it referred to the devout life or to the interior life of the individual, especially to the person's affective relationship with God. The term became controversial when the affective dimension of *spiritualité* was associated with less than orthodox enthusiastic and quietistic developments. This led to some pejorative references to *spiritualité* in contrast to devotion, which appeared to stress a more sedate human cooperation in the spiritual life. Bossuet and Voltaire, for example, attacked the "*nouvelle spiritualité*" of Madame Guyon and Fénelon as an amusement for the idle rich, particularly widows. It is probably due to this ambivalence about *spiritualité* that its use became rare in French Roman Catholic circles by the end of the eighteenth century.[22]

Traces of English devotional use of spirituality referring to piety and the devout life continued into the nineteenth century, when the word became archaic except for its occasional use in free religious groups outside the mainline churches. Within eighteenth-century Catholic theology, *spiritualité* acquired an elitist sense that distinguished the life of perfection as pursued in religious orders from the ordinary life of faith practiced by the laity. By the nineteenth century, it referred almost exclusively to the vowed life, to the practice

---

21. Principe, "Toward Defining Spirituality," 132.
22. Ibid. Also Alexander, "What Do Recent Writers Mean?" 248-49, comments that a variety of words were used in the seventeenth and eighteenth centuries to express "being spiritual," including "devotion" in Francis de Sales and the Anglican mystic William Law, "perfection" in John Wesley and the early Methodists, and "piety" among Evangelicals.

of the interior life by those seeking perfection in religious communities.

In the early decades of the twentieth century, the term *spiritualité* was revived among Roman Catholic authors in France, and the word *spirituality* gradually reentered English through translations of these French works. This restoration was closely tied to the debate among theologians at the time concerning the nature of the spiritual life. The term *spirituality* was favored over spiritual theology as a more comprehensive term by those who emphasized the continuity between the ordinary (ascetical) and extraordinary (mystical) dimensions of Christian life.[23] Use of the term *spirituality* was also tied to the effort to distinguish between dogmatic theology and the study of the spiritual life with an increasing emphasis on experience and religious consciousness.[24]

By the 1950s, the word *spirituality* had become increasingly more common in English usage than earlier terms, including *spiritual teaching, spiritual life, devout life, interior life,* and *piety.* Until the Second Vatican Council, however, Catholic use of the term *spirituality* continued to refer almost

---

23. Schneiders, "Theology and Spirituality," 263, notes that in the debate on the discontinuity or continuity of the mystical state with previous states of spiritual development, A. A. Tanquerey and R. Garrigou-Lagrange respectively represent the two contrasting views. Both authors were widely read in seminaries and novitiates prior to the Second Vatican Council.

24. Principe, "Toward Defining Spirituality," 134-45 n. 43, notes that although the pejorative sense of *spiritualité* waned, the dualistic connotation endured until very recently and in some cases still holds. General reference works have only recently begun to reflect the changing attitude. Principe finds that a broader definition of *spiritualité* was first given in a dictionary of the French language in 1964. Also, the German language was slower in using *Spiritualität* in place of *Frömmigkeit.* It first appeared in 1958 in works by Hans Urs von Balthasar and F. Wulf.

exclusively to the spiritual life of members of religious orders.

The effort in twentieth-century Roman Catholic theology toward the recovery of original sources in scripture, history, and liturgy served to correct the distortions that had arisen in many of the previous understandings of spirituality.[25] The Second Vatican Council formalized the theological and pastoral developments that had moved Roman Catholic thought from an emphasis on an incorporeal soul to a concept of the whole person, from a focus on doctrine to a sense of history, from a strictly logical to a theological method, and from a focus on first principles to the significance of experience. As a result, the post-conciliar perspective on spirituality broadened to include once again not only the vertical, prayer-oriented dimensions but also the horizontal, social dimensions of the Christian life. In particular, the Council's recognition of the value of all states of life and the laity's role in the mission of the Church, generated a holistic understanding of spirituality, reversing the long-standing emphasis on "withdrawal from the world."[26]

Since the Council, authors have also used the term *spirituality* in reference to various particular spiritualities. Studies have appeared, for instance, on the spirituality of individuals, biblical spirituality, liturgical spirituality, and the spirituality of different periods of history and various Chris-

---

25. Conn, *Spirituality and Personal Maturity* (Mahwah: Paulist, 1989), 13. Principe, "Toward Defining Spirituality," 129, notes that changes in several journal titles reflected the new understanding of spirituality, for instance in 1977 *Cross and Crown* became *Spirituality Today.*

26. Austin Flannery, O.P., in "Vatican Council II," *New Dictionary of Catholic Spirituality*, 991-97, outlines the influence of the Council on Roman Catholic spirituality. See also Conn, *Spirituality and Personal Maturity*, 25-29. Of particular relevance are the conciliar documents: "Constitution on the Church," art. 40, 41; "Missions," art. 2, and the "Decree on the Apostolate of the Laity."

tian groups. The term has also been extended to studies of non-Christian groups, for example, to Hindu or Buddhist spirituality. As might be expected, this sudden explosion in the use of the term has led to a certain degree of confusion.

Contemporary Use of Christian Spirituality

In her effort to clarify the contemporary use of the phrase *Christian spirituality*, Schneiders turns to the medieval distinction between philosophical and religious definitions of spirituality. The philosophical meaning refers to "the experience of consciously striving to integrate one's life in terms not of isolation and self absorption but of self-transcendence toward the ultimate value one perceives."[27] This definition encompasses both religious and non-religious experience while embracing the essential elements of conscious effort, life integrating self-transcendence, and a horizon of ultimate value. Schneiders observes that among both Catholic and Protestant authors,

> virtually everyone talking about spirituality today is talking about self-transcendence which gives integrity and meaning to the whole of life and to life in its wholeness by situating and orienting the person within the horizon of ultimacy in some ongoing and transforming way.[28]

The religious meaning of spirituality, on the other hand, emphasizes that the relationship with God is the proper and highest actualization of the human capacity for self-transcendence in personal relationships. Schneiders notes that Christian spirituality, as a specification of the religious mean-

---

27. Schneiders, "Theology and Spirituality," 266, and "Spirituality in the Academy," 684.

28. Schneiders, "Theology and Spirituality," 266.

ing, designates the ultimate horizon as "God revealed in Jesus Christ and experienced through the gift of the Holy Spirit within the life of the Church."[29] This description clearly identifies the essential trinitarian, christological, and ecclesial dimensions of Christian spirituality.

Schneiders also distinguishes between theological approaches to spirituality that present doctrinal or dogmatic approaches using a "definition from above" and those that present an anthropological position providing a "definition from below."[30]This distinction hinges on the underlying concept of the breadth of the field encompassed by spirituality. In Schneiders' words:

> For the dogmatic approach spirituality is the life derived from grace and therefore any experience which is not explicitly Christian can be called spirituality only by way of extension or comparison. Being human merely supplies the conditions for the reception of grace. For the anthropological approach the structure and dynamics of the human person as such are the locus of the emergence of the spiritual life. Spirituality is an activity of human life as such. . . . In principle it is equally available to every human being who is seeking to live an authentically human life.[31]

A survey of current authors indicates that the phrase *Christian spirituality* is being used predominantly in an experiential and broad sense, and in an anthropological rather than in a dogmatic sense. In other words, Christian spirituality is broadly recognized today as part of a larger concept that is not confined to or defined by Christianity or even by religion.

---

29. Schneiders, ibid., and "Spirituality in the Academy," 684.
30. Schneiders, "Spirituality and the Academy," 682.
31. Ibid.

In a holistic and psychologically oriented contemporary definition of spirituality, Joann Wolski Conn indicates that specifically Christian spirituality "involves the human capacity of self-knowledge, love, and commitment as it is actualized through the experience of God, in Jesus, the Christ, by the gift of the Spirit."[32] This perspective highlights the role of personal freedom and belief in spiritual development.

Other examples of recent definitions further illustrate the impact of the post-conciliar shift in theology on the perception of spirituality. In her article on the characteristics of spirituality in the United States, Carolyn Osiek defines spirituality as "the experience, reflection and articulation of the assumptions and consequences of religious faith as it is lived in a concrete situation."[33] Michael Downey emphasizes the experiential and ecclesial dimensions when he states that Christian spirituality

> describes the whole of the Christian's life as this is oriented to self-transcending knowledge, freedom, and love in light of the ultimate values and highest ideals perceived and pursued in the mystery of Jesus Christ through the Holy Spirit in the church, the community of disciples. That is to say, spirituality is concerned with everything that constitutes Christian experience, specifically the perception and pursuit of the highest ideal or goal of Christian life.[34]

Dutch feminist theologian Catherina Halkes' description of Christian spirituality particularly reflects the expanded social context of spirituality: "Christian spirituality is thus an attitude oriented towards the Holy Spirit, the Spirit of Christ inspiring us to live in justice and love, in liberty and

---

32. Conn, *Women's Spirituality: Resources for Christian Development,* 3.

33. Carolyn Osiek, "Reflections on an American Spirituality," *Spiritual Life* 22 (1976): 230.

34. Downey, "Understanding Christian Spirituality," 272.

authenticity, and, moving out from there, in availability for
God and for people."[35]

Each of these attempts to define spirituality demonstrates that today the term *spirituality* is no longer synony-
mous with interiority, subjectivity, or religiosity. It denotes
a way of being, a lifestyle which reflects what the gospel
calls discipleship. As John Heagle notes, where pre-conciliar
approaches to spirituality were typically theoretical, elitist,
otherworldly, and individualistic, the contemporary approach is intensely personal, visionary, prophetic, and incarnational: "It emphasizes personal response and interior
commitment but it radically changes the context within
which this response takes place."[36]

Some scholars have expressed concern that the use of
the term *spirituality* today has become so broad, abstract,
and generic that it has no meaning beyond a general reference to higher aspirations in human life. Alexander fore-
sees two theological difficulties arising from the separation
of spirituality from particular dogmatic and religious refer-
ents: the problem of distinguishing authentic from unauthentic spirituality and the problem of confusing abstract with
concrete realities. From another perspective, Principe expresses concern that over a period of time spirituality might
become divorced from theology.[37] On the other hand,
Schneiders does not perceive a need for concern. In her
thought,

> There is no such thing as generic spirituality or spiri-
> tuality in general. Every spirituality is necessarily his-
> torically concrete and therefore involves some

---

35. Catherina Halkes, "Feminism and Spirituality," *Spirituality Today* 40
    (1988): 226.

36. John Heagle, "A New Public Piety," *Church* 1, no. 3 (Fall 1985): 52-53.

37. Alexander, "What Do Recent Writers Mean?" 252-54; Principe, "Toward
    Defining Spirituality," 139.

thematically explicit commitments, some actual and distinct symbol system, some traditional language, in short a theoretical-linguistic framework which is integral to it and without which it cannot be meaningfully discussed at all.[38]

In Schneiders's view, using the common experience of self-transcendence and integration in terms of ultimate values encourages dialogue among people with different worldviews.

Throughout this book, Christian spirituality will be used in a contemporary sense to refer to a holistic, personal, free, and self-transcending experience of life that is enlightened by faith through the experience of God in Jesus and his message and by the power of the Spirit at work in the community of the church. Christian spirituality is understood here as a particular response to God that is expressed within a frame of Christian reference.

Various questions about the academic study of Christian spirituality, which are implicit in the discussions concerning the definition and use of the term, have also been addressed by contemporary scholars. The following section will examine the scope of the field that studies Christian spirituality and some of the discussions about its place in relationship to theology.

The Academic Study of Christian Spirituality

If the definition of the word *spirituality* and the description of the reality that it expresses are so elusive, it is not surprising that the scholarly study of spirituality, Principe's third category, is also the subject of debate. The discussion focuses on two questions: what is the proper subject matter

38. Schneiders, "Theology and Spirituality," 267.

for the field that studies Christian spirituality, and whether the study of spirituality is an independent discipline or a subcategory of theology.[39] The background of these questions is intertwined with the history of the understanding of spirituality itself.

The Study of Spirituality

Today, while differences remain, most scholars agree that the study of spirituality examines the human capacity for personal integration, within a wide context, in terms of self-transcendence toward a perceived ultimate value.[40] A majority of scholars in the area of Christian spirituality advocate an inclusive and existential content drawn from the experience of Christian life as a whole, incorporating an understanding of the person or group in a total context. This includes both the person's or tradition's theological

---

39. The 1988 American Academy of Religion Seminar on Spirituality was devoted to papers on "What Is Spirituality?" Although agreement was not reached about either the content or the discipline, some clarity was reached about the questions which need to be addressed. See Bradley C. Hanson, ed., *Modern Christian Spirituality: Methodological and Historical Essays* (Atlanta: Scholars Press, 1990), for several of the AAR papers and related essays.

40. Two well-known authors in the field of spirituality, Ewert Cousins and Bernard McGinn, present two other approaches to the content of the study of spirituality. Cousins considers the deepest dimensions of all authentic human experience to be expressions of a universal spiritual experience. McGinn, on the other hand, believes that all spirituality is mediated within particular religious traditions through language and texts. See Ewert H. Cousins, "Preface to the Series," in *Christian Spirituality I*, eds. B. McGinn and J. Meyendorff, xiii; and "What Is Christian Spirituality?" in *Modern Christian Spirituality*, ed. Bradley C. Hanson, 43. Bernard McGinn, "General Introduction," *Foundations of Mysticism*, vol. 1, *The Presence of God: A History of Western Christian Mysticism* (New York: Crossroad, 1991), xv.

and religious attitudes as well as the various social and cultural influences that shaped the person's or tradition's spiritual ideal and response to that ideal.

With regard to questions about the situation of spirituality within the academy, it is important to recall that until the thirteenth century, the modern division of theology into various specialized disciplines did not exist. As a unified science in which doctrine and experience were approached in a holistic manner, earlier Christian theology interpreted scripture for the purpose of understanding and living the Christian faith. The later subordination of spirituality to moral theology evolved from Thomas Aquinas's placement of his discussion of Christian experience, the essence of spirituality, in the second part of the *Summa Theologiae*, which addresses the moral life of Christians. Separate treatises on spiritual theology flourished in the wake of the highly systematic, abstract, and technical approach to theology that prevailed from the end of the thirteenth century. At the same time, the more personal writings of medieval mystics and scholars, both male and female, contributed to the body of spiritual literature.

The Reformation led to new understandings of the spiritual life in both Protestant and Catholic theological teaching. This period influenced later Roman Catholic spirituality primarily through the Spanish writers whose insights on the soul's relationship to God sprang from their own religious experience. Teresa of Avila described the deepening of the interior life of prayer. John of the Cross focused on mystical development, particularly the dark night experience. Combining action and prayer, Ignatius of Loyola drew up guidelines for spiritual growth in the midst of apostolic activities.

With the rise of the new science in the seventeenth century, the gap between daily life and the spiritual life widened, as did the split between the systematic theologians and the spiritual writers. As a consequence, personal piety became increasingly privatized and deprived of a theological base. Eventually, private devotions and popular religion developed as the laity's ordinary experience of Christianity. Due to the intense interest in the "life of perfection" and the accompanying debates that flourished in the seventeenth century, a new field of study developed in Roman Catholic theology during the eighteenth and nineteenth centuries. Labelled "spiritual theology," it described the spiritual life lived by those who had progressed beyond the basic Christian duty to keep the commandments. This science was later divided into "ascetical theology," which detailed the exercises which every Christian aspiring to perfection should adopt, and "mystical theology," which studied mystical union and its manifestations.

Although spiritual theology was understood as a branch of theology, in practice it was subordinated both to dogmatic theology from which it drew its principles and to moral theology of which it was considered a subdivision concerned with Christian life beyond the basic Christian obligations. The seminary textbooks of the early twentieth century represent the final stage of this process prior to the midcentury theological developments, which resulted in a new discipline distinct from its seminary predecessor.

In examining the history of the study of spirituality, it is important to recall that a large part of the literature on the spiritual life across the centuries was composed in extremely different genres, ranging from scriptural commentaries, sermons, and religious rules, through biographies and histories, to poems and hymns. Many of these works were written outside the schools by non-professional theologians, including the early desert writers, Benedict, Francis, Julian of Norwich, Catherine of Siena, Teresa of Avila, Ignatius, and Thérèse of Lisieux. Great classics in spirituality were also produced by Orthodox and Protestant spiritual guides.

During the nineteenth and twentieth centuries, the letters and writings of the founders of apostolic congregations of women frequently expressed the practical spiritual wisdom of pioneers. More recently, Pierre Teilhard de Chardin, Simone Weil, Thomas Merton, and Dorothy Day are among those who, through their responses to twentieth-century issues, have contributed to the literature of spirituality. The existence of works on spirituality from both theological and experiential perspectives emphasizes the dynamic relationship between theology and Christian spirituality. Since Christian spirituality refers both to lived Christian experience and to a field of study, this relationship has two dimensions. On the one hand, as lived religious experience, Christian spirituality influences both the content and the style of theology because human experience is the primary source for theology. Spiritual traditions are initially embodied in people rather than doctrine and grow out of life rather than from abstract ideas. As liberation theologian Gustavo Gutiérrez notes, "At the outset of every spirituality there lies a personal experience of the Lord. A spirituality is not the application of theology. What happens is rather that a spiritual approach is followed by a reflection on faith as it is lived in this perspective, a theology."[41] At the same time, the experiential perspective also acts as a critical balance for theology when it becomes too abstract and separated from ordinary life.

Theology, on the other hand, grounds particular spiritualities and the study of spirituality in the Christian tradition, which both shapes and critiques their direction and development.[42] For example, contemporary spirituality in the

---

41. Gustavo Gutiérrez, "Drink from Your Own Well," in *Learning to Pray* (Concilium 159), ed. C. Floristán and C. Duquoc (New York: Seabury, 1982), 40.

42. For discussions of the relationship between spirituality and theology, see, among others, Annice Callahan, "The Relationship between

United States has been influenced by theologians from around the world, including Karl Rahner, Bernard Lonergan, Pierre Teilhard de Chardin, and Gustavo Gutiérrez. The insights of feminist theologians such as Rosemary Radford Ruether and Elisabeth Schüssler-Fiorenza and of ecological theologians such as Sallie McFague have provided the bases for a feminist and ecologically sensitive contemporary spirituality.

Although agreement has not been reached on many questions, the contemporary study of Christian spirituality is flourishing. While spirituality as a discipline is still finding its way, the methods and content of recent books and journals on Christian spirituality demonstrate a number of trends in this field. As Jesuit Philip Sheldrake observes, "Contemporary spirituality is characterized more by an attempt to integrate human and religious values than by an exclusive interest in the component parts of 'spiritual' growth such as stages of prayer."[43]

From her research in the field, Sandra Schneiders finds that contemporary studies in spirituality are characteristically interdisciplinary, descriptive, and critical rather than prescriptive and normative. They are also ecumenical, interreligious, and cross-cultural. She also points to the important triple finality of the discipline of spirituality, which aims toward not only the development of knowledge but also the enrichment of the researchers' own spiritual lives and through them the spiritual lives of others.[44]

Spirituality and Theology," *Horizons* 16 (1989): 267-73; Ewert H. Cousins, "Spirituality: A Resource for Theology"; Regina Bechtle, "Convergences in Theology and Spirituality," *The Way* 25 (1985): 305-14. Donal Dorr, *Spirituality and Justice* (Maryknoll: Orbis, 1984), 25, notes that theology not only gives expression but also order to belief and experience.

43. Sheldrake, *Contemporary Spirituality*, 51.

44. Schneiders, "Theology and Spirituality," 268-69; and "Spirituality in

In summarizing the trends she finds in contemporary studies in spirituality, Joann Wolski Conn points to

> [the] sustained attention to feminist issues, concern for the link between prayer and social justice, reliance on classical sources for answers to current questions, recognition of the value of developmental psychology and its understanding of "the self," and agreement that experience is the most appropriate starting point.[45]

Each of these trends frequently includes several others. For example, both Mary Jo Weaver's and Anne Carr's descriptions of feminist spirituality stress women's experience, emphasize the relationship between personal and social religious response, refer to classical sources, and recognize the contributions of developmental psychology.[46] In *Gaia and God* Rosemary Ruether draws on biblical, historical, theological, feminist, and ecological insights to describe earth healing through an ecological spirituality.

The multifaceted contemporary approach to spirituality is also evident in efforts to identify characteristic elements of Christian spiritualities in various cultural settings. For instance, in her essay on spirituality in the U.S. context, Osiek identifies an attitude of simplicity rather than austerity, of appreciation for the constructive use of power, of equality between men and women, of cultural pluralism, and of an implicit operational theology which critiques the theoretical with the experiential, as characteristic of American spirituality.[47] Kathleen Fischer believes that today's expanded

---

the Academy," 692-95.

45. Conn, *Spirituality and Personal Maturity*, 31; and also "Horizons on Contemporary Spirituality."

46. Mary Jo Weaver, *New Catholic Women: A Contemporary Challenge to Traditional Religious Authority* (San Francisco: Harper and Row, 1985), 211-12. Carr, *Transforming Grace*, 201-14.

47. Osiek, "Reflections on an American Spirituality," 30-40. See also two

worldview challenges us to make inclusiveness a key dimension in a renewed spirituality in which solidarity and compassion are central virtues.[48]

Outside the Western European and English-speaking North American contexts, Latin American theologians describe spirituality today within the whole agenda of Christian life in their situations where poverty and oppression are everyday realities.[49] They focus on liberation and justice as constitutive elements of Christian spirituality. Third World feminist theologians add an important voice to the discussion through their descriptions and analyses of the spirituality emerging among women in circumstances of poverty, sexism, racism, and political oppression.[50]

---

volumes edited by Francis Eigo, *Dimensions of Contemporary Spirituality* (Villanova: Villanova University Press, 1982), and *Contemporary Spirituality: Responding to the Divine Initiative* (Villanova: Villanova University Press, 1983).

48. Kathleen Fischer, *Reclaiming the Connections: A Contemporary Spirituality* (Kansas City, Mo.: Sheed & Ward, 1990), 10-11.

49. Gutiérrez, *We Drink from Our Own Wells*, emphasizes the inner personal and ecclesial sources of spirituality. Jon Sobrino, *Christianity at the Crossroads* (New York: Orbis, 1978), stresses the priority of praxis in Christian spirituality. Both authors consider the preferential option for the poor essential to Christian spirituality in their context of living among the oppressed.

50. See, for example, Virginia Fabella and Mercy Amba Oduyoye, eds., *With Passion and Compassion: Third World Women Doing Theology* (Maryknoll: Orbis, 1988), which presents reflections by the Women's Commission of the Ecumenical Association of Third World Theologians (EATWOT). Also, Virginia Fabella, Peter K. H. Lee, and David Kwang-sun Suh, eds., *Asian Christian Spirituality: Reclaiming Traditions* (Maryknoll: Orbis, 1992).

Conclusion

This chapter has examined the long and sometimes complex history of spirituality, both as a term and as a concept addressed on the levels of personal experience, spiritual teaching, and scholarly study. Although the various discussions continue, it is possible to summarize the present situation. Conn incorporates the multiple dimensions of the topic when she writes:

> Spirituality today refers both to lived experience and to an academic discipline. The latter is past the initial stage in which scholars develop some common vocabulary, basic categories, and journals for publication. Yet it has not reached the mature point at which it has the generalized theory that would enable it to be a developed discipline fully recognized in academic circles. Spirituality is in the fascinating intermediate stage in which it creates its new identity while remaining linked to its family of origin.[51]

In this study of Rosemary Haughton as a resource for a hope-filled contemporary Christian spirituality, spirituality is taken in the inclusive and anthropological sense suggested by Schneiders, both with reference to the lived experience and to the study of spirituality. This approach to spirituality is reflected in the organization of the book, which presents a biographical sketch of Rosemary Haughton before examining her theological perspectives and taking up her understanding and lived expression of a contemporary Christian spirituality.

---

51. Conn, *Spirituality and Personal Maturity*, 29.

Chapter Two

Searching for "Something Important"
Rosemary Haughton:
A Biographical Sketch

Suddenly there flared up in my mind a great longing which I had known before, obscurely, but which I could now identify more nearly. I wanted to know this "important something," this thing that lived between the candles and the statues and in which the black-shawled women immersed themselves. I was filled with a curiosity so strong that it was more like being extremely hungry than like merely wanting information.

      – Rosemary Haughton, "Something Important"[1]

Rosemary Haughton's theology and spirituality flow from her experience as a child growing up in England from the late 1920s through the war years; as a wife, mother, author, and lecturer in the post-war period and Vatican II era; and since 1981, as a member of the Wellspring Community, which offers shelter and resources to homeless women and families and to many other low income and poor people, through education, housing and economic development. Since Haughton's theology is, as she describes it, a "theology of experience," it is important to preface a study of her

---

1. Rosemary Haughton, "Something Important," *Sign* 57, no. 5 (February 1978): 17.

theology and spirituality with a sketch of her life and the contexts in which it has unfolded.[2]

A "Moveable" Childhood (1927-1940)

Rosemary Luling Haughton was born in Chelsea, near London, on April 13, 1927, the eldest of three daughters born to Peter Dunham Luling and his wife, Sylvia Thompson. Although her father was born in the United States, he was raised mainly in England. Haughton's mother was a British novelist of Jewish descent. Her sister Elizabeth, two years younger, was Rosemary's childhood companion and rival. The paths of their adult lives, however, separated them for many years. Elizabeth died in childbirth in 1963, before the sisters had time to develop an adult relationship. In her early years, Virginia, their much younger sister, experienced Rosemary more as her extra mother than her sister. In adulthood, Rosemary and Virginia have become and remain close friends.

Rosemary's paternal grandparents, of American stock and Episcopalian, were cultured New Yorkers who enjoyed gracious living and appreciated the arts. Grandfather Luling was the spoilt only son of a wealthy New Orleans family. Grandmother Grace Lathrop Dunham had studied piano under the renowned Ignace Paderewski. Together they entertained many literary and artistic figures of the day. Portraits of members of the family were painted by the noted American artist John Singer Sargent. A journalist once described the Lulings as "Americans of the sort found in the pages of

---

2. In addition to the noted sources, the material for this biographical sketch is taken from my correspondence and conversations with Rosemary Haughton and from a draft of an autobiography, intended for circulation among the family, to which she graciously gave me access during my stay at Wellspring House in February, 1993.

Henry James's novels, who annually spent some time in England and finally decided to settle there, in Wimbledon."[3] Memories of visits to her American grandparents over several years of childhood and adolescence remained with Rosemary:

> I loved to visit my grandparents' house. . . . [where] meals were served with the formality of a lace-aproned parlor-maid, where tea was in the library with cucumber sandwiches and tiny cakes, or out on the lawn under the big cedar. . . . Because my ordinary life was erratic and comparatively unstructured, I welcomed this especially "concentrated" kind of routine, which other children might have found restrictive, just as an undernourished person may need food concentrates.[4]

As Haughton indicates in her recollections, her parents' lives differed from those of her grandparents. Despite, or perhaps because of, his structured upbringing, her father became an impulsive, though sensitive and intelligent, adult. Though a talented water-color artist, he was remembered by his children in their early years primarily for his frequent absences, which limited his influence on his daughters' characters.

Haughton's mother, Sylvia Thompson Luling, a successful novelist, loved her children in her own self-centered, erratic, and distant manner. Absorbed in her writing and other interests, she periodically was unable to cope with the responsibilities of parenthood. She often relegated these tasks to her own mother, who ultimately played the major role in the Luling children's early development.

Depending upon the success of Sylvia Thompson Luling's publishing ventures and how quickly she spent the

---

3. Arthur Jones, "One Woman's Progress," *The Tablet* 238 (28 January 1984): 79-80.

4. Rosemary Haughton, "The Routines of Life," *The Catholic World* 212 (November 1973): 64.

proceeds, the family's lifestyle fluctuated. During good times, the family and nanny or nursery governess travelled to Paris, Venice, Switzerland, the Riviera, or the United States. In leaner times, they retreated to rented cottages in the English countryside or by the sea. Frequently, they simply returned to grandmother Ethel Thompson's house.

Haughton's maternal grandmother, Ethel Hannah Levis Thompson, came from a Jewish family, although not an observant one. Her family, successful and cultured people, were involved in tea and rubber enterprises. Ethel was educated at Somerville College, Oxford. Rebelling against her family's affluent lifestyle, she had married against their wishes into what she thought to be a typically proper English family, only to discover that her husband was neither successful nor faithful. Refusing to live on the charity of her wealthy and much older sisters, Ethel proved herself an independent survivor as a divorced single parent of two children in the reserved Edwardian milieu of the early 1900s. Ethel's struggles made her very aware of the social issues affecting women and developed in her a strong self-discipline and persistence, qualities which she passed on to the young Rosemary.

During her years as a young child, Rosemary was unaware of the unrest in both her parents' personal lives and in the broader cultural and political world. Her earliest memories describe a happy although unconventional, sometimes affluent, English upbringing of the period, complete with white pinafores and ever watchful nannies. In retrospect, Haughton describes her parents as part of the post-World War I cosmopolitan and artistic scene that was centered in Paris and overflowed onto the Riviera. Her parents dealt with their frequent marital upheavals by living in France, more or less together, but with other interests and attachments to enliven things. As a consequence of their parents' rather Bohemian lifestyle, the children moved frequently, attended school irregularly, and were exposed to a broad range of experiences.

When the family income dwindled below the nanny-and-governess level, the girls spent long periods with Ethel Thompson, who remained the center of their universe and provided a much needed creative freedom within a structured home life. Haughton says emphatically, "This courageous, intelligent, energetic and curiously innocent woman of passionate loyalties was the most important influence in my early years." She provided Rosemary and Elizabeth with the only consistent affection and security in their otherwise unpredictable childhood. With her encouragement, the girls' imaginations soared.

> Her strictness, attempting to give shape to our lives amid the chaos of our parents' undirected life-style, made stringent demands on us, her punishments were swift and her justice inexorable, but on Sunday mornings we crept into her big bed to listen to stories, sip Earl Grey tea and nibble "Digestive" biscuits, which she kept in a jar with large cabbage roses on it. Her taste in books, her enthusiasms and dreams were passed on to us.[5]

At the same time, at Ethel's house the girls were allowed to exchange their prim dresses for overalls and to explore the wonders of trees and puddles.

Granny's influence continued even during the journeys abroad for, as Haughton recalls, "During these adventures, the long arm of Granny's nursery discipline pursued us in the form of a succession of nannies and governesses of varying efficiency." Ethel Thompson also enforced high ideals of intellectual attainment and a fierce drilling in self-control and courtesy. Haughton also remembers her grand-

---

5. Rosemary Haughton, autobiography, unpublished manuscript.

mother as a born teacher who imparted to her a passion
for delving into historical matters that has only grown with
time.

Although her parents attended church irregularly,
mainly for Christmas services and on special occasions,
Haughton recounts that the need to discover God became
clear to her at a very early age. At first she encountered
the things of God through stories and pictures of saints. She
made her first tentative explorations of a Roman Catholic
church, at age five, in the company of a Catholic friend of
the family who took her and Elizabeth for walks on the
beach and bought them ice creams. When they visited the
local church, the candles, aromas, and glimpses of gilt and
colors gleaming in the candlelight made a profound impres-
sion on the young Rosemary. "It wasn't just what I could
see that remained in my mind; I also retained what can only
be described as a sense of 'something important.' Being in
that place seemed to matter."[6]

Three years later, when Rosemary's mother spent some
months in Venice in late summer 1934, their English nanny
felt it was important for the children to see the art in various
Venetian churches. Once again Rosemary experienced the
dimly lit statues and the dancing candles, which "burned
together, in a mysterious exchange of life."

> Suddenly there flared up in my mind a great longing
> which I had known before, obscurely, but which I
> could now identify more nearly. I wanted to know this
> "important something," this thing that lived between
> the candles and the statues and in which the black-
> shawled women immersed themselves. I was filled
> with a curiosity so strong that it was more like being

---

6. Haughton, "Something Important," 16.

extremely hungry than like merely wanting information.[7]

In recalling this experience, Haughton comments that "it
was in Venice, in fact, that a curiosity about religion, a
secret but deep need to know, began to stir in me." This
intense curiosity remained characteristic of her ongoing
search for the meaning of the "important something."

In her early years, this gentle but insistent call continued
for Rosemary almost entirely through the lives of the saints,
which she devoured from books given to her by her devout
Anglican godmother. She lived through those stories in a
world that seemed more real and important than the dull
world of school or the routines of daily life:

> I knew nothing of Christian doctrine except garbled
> snatches absorbed at random during services, and I told
> no one of my passion. It was through the saints, my
> companions, my friends, my models, that I touched the
> reality of God's Kingdom. What better way could there
> be to discover it? There were no doctrines or explanation,
> only people who lived by these doctrines and whose
> loveliness witnessed better than any explanation.[8]

On visits to her American grandparents, Rosemary regularly
accompanied her grandmother to Episcopalian services and
Evensong. She recalls that

> from the colored glass and windows, from the hymns
> and the half-understood readings I wove fantasies and
> daydreams. I made a private kingdom whose inhabi-
> tants were Jesus and his friends living in a bright
> garden, speaking of strange and glorious deeds.[9]

---

7. Ibid., 17.
8. Haughton, "The Saints," 31.
9. Ibid., 30.

It bothered Rosemary, however, that all these saints lived so long ago, for there were no modern Catholic saints in her Anglican books! What a happy surprise it was for her when a friend introduced her to St. Thérèse of Lisieux (1873-1897). The photograph of a little girl of not so long ago sitting on her father's knee astounded Rosemary. This was a saint? A little girl like those in her family picture albums? Somehow, that photograph broke into Rosemary's fantasy world with the message, "God belongs in our time, and in the ordinary world."

After spending the summer of 1936 in a sixteenth-century English cottage in Romney Marsh, near Rye, the two girls and their mother spent the fall in New York, in a wonderful apartment overlooking Central Park. When money ran out, an inexpensive apartment in the Berkshires in Massachusetts took its place for a few months. The winter of 1938-1939, the last winter before the war, found the girls in Gstaad, Switzerland, with their mother and grandmother Ethel. The family group returned to England, to Ethel's house in Kent, in time for Virginia's birth in June 1939.

The next move was to a cottage in Hertsfordshire with both parents from late summer 1939 until just after war was declared. During the war the family was unable to return to Ethel's house because it was too near the coast and all the local people had been evacuated. For this reason, a time of wandering began, during which the Lulings stayed with relatives or in briefly rented homes. While he was waiting to get into the armed forces, Peter Luling served on rescue teams in London. After he joined the military, he was posted at the War Office in London.

Embracing Catholicism: Teenage Years
(1940-1948)

Rosemary's teenage years were shaped by the austerities and uncertainty of wartime England, which included food rationing, air-raid alerts, evacuation, demolished buildings, and disrupted transportation systems. Since her mother had Jewish distant cousins, who had narrowly escaped from Austria before the frontiers were closed, the family realized what might happen to them if Hitler's troops crossed the English Channel. Meanwhile, even in the shadows of war, the Luling family life continued in its characteristically impetuous and unconventional patterns.

Rosemary's naturally insatiable desire for knowledge in general and about God in particular persisted. She and Elizabeth attended Benenden School, a boarding school that had been evacuated from Kent to a vacant hotel in Newquay, Cornwall. While there in 1940, she asked to learn Greek. Later that year, during a long convalescence at school during a measles epidemic, she rejoiced in the opportunity to read without the interruptions of the regular schedule.

During this time, Rosemary's search for meaning and direction in her life continued, and at times even permeated her daily activities. As she matured, her earlier childish searchings became both more intense and more frustrating because there was nobody with whom to discuss her thoughts and feelings. When she heard that a Confirmation class was forming at school, she quickly asked to enroll, believing that here, perhaps, was the key to understanding the mystery of life. In her mind, "Those who were confirmed, were, I knew, full members of the church, they could go to Communion. When I could do that, I felt I would have the key."

Rosemary's request was greeted with suspicion by her teachers and grandmother. After all, sixteen was the usual age for Confirmation, and she was only thirteen. Did she simply want a new dress? Was she competing with her classmates? Was she unwell? Had her parents suggested this? In the end, she was admitted to the weekly classes held by the local vicar. Recalling this episode, Haughton states that, although she would not have used the words then, she really was seeking to enter more fully into the Christian mystery.

Up to this point, her grandmother's commonsense approach to Christianity was Rosemary's only source of religion apart from books and church services. Ethel's religion emphasized personal moral responsibility, especially honesty. Jesus, if mentioned, was the example and guide for a good life. On the other hand, the very high church vicar stressed grace and redemption, and the sacraments, all new concepts to Rosemary. She readily accepted his explanations of the Church of England as the true heir of the medieval church and the true Catholic Church. Although she longed for heroism and personal spiritual experience rather than institutional church life, she still hoped that the sacrament of Confirmation and above all the reception of Holy Communion would reveal to her what she wanted to know.

The day after Confirmation, the class went to the early service to receive Holy Communion. A profoundly disillusioned Rosemary discovered that she had not changed. "I went to breakfast the same person as I got up that morning," she recalls. Although she did not admit it to anyone, she thought that God, at least the Anglican one, had let her down.

The long darkness and cold of the winter of 1940-1941 continued. Its harshness was deepened by wartime economy measures and concern about Virginia who had developed pneumonia while they spent the Christmas holidays with friends in a large cold house. For a while, Rosemary and Elizabeth stayed with their great-aunt, Ethel's sister Cecile, a deaf but benevolent tyrant with a large house in Reigate, Surrey. There the two girls entertained themselves, with the help of an old family friend who was an actress, by learning and performing some two-character scenes from Shakespeare, including Celia and Rosalind from *As You Like It* and Viola and Olivia in *Twelfth Night.* At night, the girls could see the air raids on London light up the sky.

In the summer of 1941, the family moved to a rented cottage, and later to Aldershot, to a big Victorian house which they rented for three years. During this period, Rosemary and Elizabeth attended Farnham Girls Grammar School for two years, the longest period they ever spent in one school.

The local vicar, John Rowsell, his wife and sons lived next door and became good friends of the Lulings. The vicar gave Rosemary the run of his library and she eagerly explored his volumes on myth, legends, and theology. She also occasionally attended the weekday early service in the medieval Lady Chapel of his church, an experience she found peaceful and comforting. The years in Aldershot were very important ones for Rosemary, for she then developed her passion for both art and religion.

Both of these passions had a chance to develop further when Rosemary was allowed to move to London in 1942, alone, at the age of fifteen. Conscious of her daughter's developing artistic talent, her mother arranged for her to live in London during the school term with Austrian Jewish friends of Ethel Thompson. There she attended the Regent Street Polytechnic part-time while also taking regular classes at Queen's College in Harley Street. Since the air raids had ceased, at least temporarily, this arrangement seemed reasonably safe.

Rosemary had become acquainted with the Breuer family in 1938 when they had first arrived in England as refugees. Frau Kati was cheerful and motherly. For Rosemary, however, the best part of this adventure was the sense that her rented room was her private space. In reality, she recalls, it was dingy, with faded furniture and ugly wallpaper, but it was hers, her own place to spread out her art supplies and be content. She put flowerboxes in the windows and revelled in her independence.

Rosemary used her new freedom to spend time in Queen's College library, engrossed in reading books about sailing boats and copying their illustrations. Although she ate dinner in the evening with the Breuers, she had lunch by herself, usually in a tea shop while reading a book. She listened to wartime midday concerts at the empty National Gallery (the art having been removed to caves in Wales) and studied the lone exhibited "Picture of the Month" and its various accompanying sketches and explanations. She also attended the ballet, after waiting for hours for the cheapest tickets, and collected postcards of her favorite dancers.

Rosemary had never told anyone about her childhood experiences of "something important" amid the glow of candles and the smell of incense in churches. Nevertheless, she never forgot the great longing she had experienced on those occasions. As she recounts, "As I grew up, I pursued my not-only-secret but secretive search, reading lives of saints, slipping into empty churches, sitting out on the windward side of rocks where the sea spray blew, asking God to show me what I needed to know."[10] It is not surprising that one of the first things she did in London was to investigate the Roman Catholic Church.

Rosemary looked up an old Catholic friend of her mother's, Miss Barratt. Known affectionately as "Batty" by the Luling girls, she invited Rosemary to high tea in her little top floor flat in a Victorian house in Hammersmith. Rosemary asked her, the only Roman Catholic she knew, to help her learn more about Catholicism. Batty took the request seriously and introduced Rosemary to a Benedictine sister at Tyburn Convent, which stood near the site of the

---

10. Haughton, "Something Important," 18.

gallows of Tyburn where many sixteenth-century Roman Catholic martyrs had been executed.

So it was that in April 1943, Rosemary Luling met Mother Raphael, the petite and ancient nun who was to be her instructor. Rosemary appreciated the nun's understanding and the way she treated her as an adult. Mother Raphael, on her part, realized that Rosemary, although intelligent and determined, was still partly a child, and adjusted her instruction accordingly. She provided Rosemary with a curious assortment of books. Romantic historical novels about Elizabethan martyrs combined with lives of the saints. Theological classics mixed with spiritual works, including Abbot Marmion's *Christ, the Life of the Soul*, Jean-Pierre de Caussade's *Abandonment to Divine Providence*, and Francis de Sales' *Treatise on the Love of God*. She also read about Thérèse of Lisieux and the letters of the English converts Dom Chapman and Janet Erskine Stuart.[11]

On her own, Rosemary delved into the poetry of Paul Claudel and Charles Williams and the novels of Georges Bernanos and Baroness Orczy.[12] Within the next two years

---

11. Mother Raphael's reading list reflects both her tailoring of the material to her young pupil and the spiritual tastes of the period. Francis de Sales's (1567-1622) *Treatise on the Love of God* is considered a classic treatment of the laity's pursuit of holiness in everyday life. Jesuit Jean-Pierre de Caussade (1675-1751) followed the Salesian ideal of evangelical poverty. Thérèse Martin (1873-1897) entered the Carmel of Lisieux at fifteen and was canonized in 1925. John Chapman (1865-1933), ordained an Anglican priest in 1889, converted to Catholicism and was later a Benedictine historian, exegete, and abbot of Downside Abbey. His spiritual letters were published in 1935. The daughter of an Anglican rector, Janet Erskine Stuart (1857-1914) converted to Catholicism at twenty-one, entered the Society of the Sacred Heart at twenty-five, became an educator and spiritual writer, and was later superior general of the community.

12. Rosemary's choices show her thirst for role models and her love for literature. Paul Claudel (1868-1955), French dramatist, essayist, and religious poet, chose to return to Catholicism at age eighteen. Friedrich

she avidly read the letters of Teresa of Avila, Baron von Hügel's *Letters to a Niece*, a number of C. S. Lewis' stories, more Catholic novels, and even sections of Thomas Aquinas's *Summa Theologiae*. Aspects of Charles Williams' works, which she discovered at this time, would later make a significant contribution to the expression of her theological understanding. Twice a week Rosemary brought a sandwich and a book to Hyde Park. There she lay in the uncut grass (only sheep cut the grass of London's wartime parks!), ate her sandwich, and read the books she had been given, until it was time to see Mother Raphael. Her favorite reading was the biographies of saints, her old friends from childhood now in a grown-up guise. The meetings with Mother Raphael, followed by Compline and Benediction in the convent chapel, became the high points of Rosemary's week. On the weekends, back in Aldershot, she started attending Mass in the Roman Catholic church instead of participating in the services at the Church of England.

During these months of instruction, Rosemary found some of the answers to her earlier questions. She remembers that when she encountered Catholicism this time,

> I recognized, with the kind of joy that is more like fear, the same "something important" which I had discerned in an empty church at a seaside town. . . .
>
> That rediscovery was swift and enthralling and quite different, . . . But I knew that this odd religion which I had encountered was the right place to look, because

---

von Hügel (1852-1925), theologian and philosopher, is known for his *Mystical Elements of Religion* (1908). Georges Bernanos (1888-1948), a French novelist and essayist, initially wrote imaginative fiction but switched to political comment during the ominous events of the 1930s. Hungarian-born novelist Baroness Emmuska Orczy (1865-1947) married Montague Barstow and is remembered for *The Scarlet Pimpernel*. Charles Williams (1886-1945), a British author interested in the Arthurian legends, and the British essayist C. S. Lewis (1889-1963) were members of the Inklings, a literary group at Oxford.

> I already had that old, secret "touchstone" in my
> consciousness. I knew how "it" felt, and the feel of it
> was the certainty of something real, ultimate, glorious,
> and more important than anything else in the world.[13]

Gradually, her intuitive sense of God was finding expression
in a tradition.

During the summer of 1943, Rosemary joined her
mother and sisters for a holiday in Devon where she spent
the days on the beach sketching and reading more of Mother
Raphael's books. One small black book of questions and
answers about Catholicism was oddly engrossing. Years later
she remarks:

> The logic and reason was what I hungered for, for a
> mind fed too much on imagination and fantasy . . .
> the dry-as-dust arguments gave my growing mind
> something to chew on – and I was too young to realize
> how the questions were restricted to the answer that
> would fit.[14]

Rosemary indulged her religious fantasies during the holiday
by listening to the Latin hymns sung by the Poor Clare nuns
in the local church.

Later that summer, when the immediate danger from
the war seemed more remote, Rosemary's parents decided
to move back to London. She joined them in a small rented
house behind Kensington High Street. Meanwhile, she continued her instruction at Tyburn Convent.

Finally, on December 23, 1943, Rosemary was accepted
with conditional baptism into the Roman Catholic Church.
She received her First Communion as a Roman Catholic at
the Christmas Midnight Mass at Our Lady of Victories,
celebrated in a makeshift building since the church itself

---

13. Haughton, "Something Important," 18.
14. Haughton, unpublished autobiography, n.p.

had been bombed. In the weeks that followed, she walked through the dark morning streets to the Carmelite church for the candlelit early Mass. In looking back at this time, Haughton observes:

> I became a Catholic at 16, drawn to it by a conviction that at [the] heart of this curious experience called 'the church' there was to be found the possibility of an incredible richness of heroism, strangeness, beauty and a glory opening upon eternity. I never found cause to doubt this. . . .
>
> In those early years before the council I reached out hungrily, feeling my way into the age-darkened recesses of this thing I longed to understand and to love. The magic was woven of basic symbols, lights, voices in chant, ancient phrases – but at the heart of it all lay a starkness, the irreducibleness of words spoken though not heard, that had power, that touched the essential.[15]

These comments illustrate Haughton's ongoing and maturing fascination with the mystery of God and life. They also indicate the strong influence of the church on the foundation of her early theological understanding and spirituality.

The furious air raids of February 1944 prompted Rosemary's parents to move out of London once again. Elizabeth and Rosemary stayed with a family in Reigate, closer to London, so they could go up to London to school during the day, an arrangement they disliked thoroughly. Rosemary attended the Easter liturgy for the first time in the little Romanesque church in Reigate.

Shortly afterward, the girls stayed with their grandmother, who was doing war work for the Y.W.C.A. Later, her mother and youngest sister moved to a friend's house

---

15. Rosemary Haughton, "We Caught the Touch of Incarnate Love," *National Catholic Reporter* 18 (8 October 1982): 15.

further out of London and Elizabeth went to boarding school. Rosemary, then seventeen, went for one more term to the Slade School of Art, which had been evacuated to Oxford. Next she moved back to London to help her father paint and repair the large flat in Chelsea which the Lulings had decided to rent. After they moved in, she signed up with the Volunteer Aid Detachment and worked in a hospital until the end of the war.

Despite the probability of victory, London in the last year of the war endured severe shortages. At the same time, this was also a period of hope and relief. Rosemary and a small group of student and young worker friends would sometimes gather in the evenings over milkless hot chocolate in someone's shabby bed-sitter. They read poetry, discussed plays or the ballet, and talked about God, the medieval mystics, the new lay movements, and the vocation of Christians in the world. She remembers those days vividly:

> We shared with everyone else around us the common discomforts and dangers, but our Christian vocation shed a greater light on the opportunities of that common situation. The natural buoyancy and camaraderie of the nation, as it emerged from five years of uncertainty and fear, were transmuted, by the knowledge of Christ, into something greater – a joy in poverty voluntarily accepted, a sense of dedication to a cause which transcended material prosperity, a hope for the making of a future in accordance with Gospel ideals, a gratitude to God for the pleasure of companionship in Christ, of plans made and work undertaken because of him.[16]

After the war as an art student in Paris, Rosemary experienced the wave of solidarity and resurgent faith evi-

---

16. Rosemary Haughton, *In Search of Tomorrow: A Future to Believe In* (St. Meinrad, Ind.: Abbey Press, 1972), 53-54.

dent in the Young Christian Students groups. Long before the Second Vatican Council and amid post-war shortages, hope, and idealism, she was introduced to dialogue Masses and liturgies with the priest facing the people. A war-weary people saw new needs and new possibilities for the Christian community as the people of God around a table, with baptism as birth into a new society.

Haughton's later writings indicate that during these years in Paris she became familiar with the work of Jacques Maritain, Gabriel Marcel, Charles Péguy, Etienne Gilson, and Maurice Blondel.[17] Many of these Christian philosophical and social ideals, which she first experienced in the Christian communities of post-war Paris, became important influences on her later life and work.

---

17. A survey of these authors reveals the influence of Haughton's early philosophical and literary reading on her later interests and activities: Maurice Blondel (1861-1949), a French philosopher, sought to revitalize Catholic thought and hoped to bridge intellectualism and pragmatism. Etienne Gilson (1884-1978) was a French philosopher associated with the twentieth-century revival in medieval studies. Gabriel Marcel (1889-1973), French philosopher, dramatist, and critic, and convert to Roman Catholicism, was a Christian existentialist. Jacques Maritain (1882-1973), also a convert, was a widely known Catholic philosopher who supported neo-Thomism and also admired English romantic poetry. Charles Péguy (1871-1914) was a fiercely patriotic French essayist, dramatist, and poet, whose deeply personalist philosophy combined socialism, patriotism, and Catholicism.

Marriage and Family Building: Yorkshire Years
(1948-1973)

After her return to London, Rosemary Luling shared a flat with Jennifer Jennings, the daughter of the headmaster at a local school. In time, Jennifer introduced Rosemary to E. Algernon Haughton, who was teaching at her father's school during the period between his demobilization from the British Navy and the start of his studies at Downing College, Cambridge.

Born in New Jersey in 1923 to an Irish father and an English mother, Algy Haughton was raised in a very strict evangelical sect, the Plymouth Brethren. After his mother died, when he was fourteen, his father moved the family to England to be near other relatives. When Algy became interested in Roman Catholicism during his time in the Navy, his only sister disassociated herself from him. Rosemary describes Algy as a good teacher and friend, a gregarious but sensitive person who dislikes introspection.

Rosemary Luling and Algy Haughton were married in London, at Westminster Cathedral, on June 19, 1948, after his first year at the university. Just two years after their marriage, when Algy had finished his abbreviated degree in English at Cambridge, the young couple tested their idealism. They embarked upon their first community experiment by founding a family-style school for boys and girls in Wales. When the project collapsed from a shortage of both capital and experience, they were left without home or job and with three babies, including twins, and another baby on the way. In addition, Peter, one of their former students at the school and son of a homeless widow, stayed with them during his school vacation, and continued to do so until he was grown.

A series of misfortunes ensued, including financial difficulties and living in various trailer homes and a horribly furnished rented place. Eventually, the young family's situation improved when Algy Haughton obtained a permanent teaching post at the Benedictine College in Ampleforth, Yorkshire. In her autobiographical notes, Haughton comments that through these various ups and downs, she and Algy were developing a conviction about the importance of saying yes to life, and learning to welcome whatever happened. Their desire to assist young people work out their problems remained with them and as a result their home frequently became a refuge for those in need.

On one occasion, with eight of their own children, the Haughtons cared for five children from another family so their mother could cope more easily with the three sick little ones who remained with her. The visitors promptly developed whooping cough, and stayed considerably longer than the planned vacation time. Later, on a referral by the Sisters of Charity in Newcastle, the Haughtons took in a brother and sister aged nine and ten as foster children during vacation periods. Two years later, these children asked if they could stay all year round, and an official foster-care was arranged. Eventually, the brother and sister remained with the Haughton family until they were grown up.

Haughton recalls that this all added up to a home that was usually overcrowded and short of money. At the same time, she did not see her family as a closed circle but as a Christian household in the Pauline sense, a Christian family community, a center for those in need. Reviewing the impact of their early attempts at Christian community, Haughton writes:

> It seems to me that, pushed by a mixture of circumstances, principle and temperament, we have stumbled onto a form of Christian life which could provide the typical form of the church's work and life in the immediate future. . . . For what we are involved in is not so much a family, in the now traditional Western

sense, as a *household*, of the kind we come across in St. Paul's letters, and which were the nuclei of the new "churches." This is a variable community of people based on, and given stability by, the central family group, but providing a welcome to all kinds of people, and not only those in need, but Christians with ideas to share or projects to discuss.[18]

Although circumstances sometimes forced a tempering of the Haughtons' idealism, their belief in the possibility of an open Christian family persisted, and hospitality became a way of life for them.

During the years in Yorkshire, Rosemary worked with Algy in many of his activities at the Benedictine college, especially the drama program which he directed. She helped with the stage and costume design. In addition, she frequently made all the costumes and took care of choreography when it was needed. She believes that some of their best times were when they worked on these productions together.

Throughout their parenting years, the Haughtons were always concerned about how education influenced their children's developing value systems. At one point, dissatisfied with the situation in the overcrowded village school, Rosemary undertook to teach their children at home. Occasional chaos resulted from eight students between the ages of five and thirteen as well as an occasionally disruptive two-year-old. Even so, she felt the children were getting a better education than they would have received in the village school. When a new school was built, the younger children enrolled and the older ones went on to other schools. In retrospect, Haughton comments, "It was an interesting, if stressful, experiment."

---

18. Rosemary Haughton, "Blueprint for a Family-Centered Community," *Marriage* 52, no. 3 (March 1970): 57.

Notwithstanding all these activities, Haughton was also busy writing in order to supplement the family income. Although raised in a literary household, she began her writing career by chance. In 1954, she was invited to illustrate a children's book on St. Thérèse being written by a community of Carmelite nuns. When the authors were unable to finish the book, they asked Haughton to complete the text as well. She went on both to write and to illustrate numerous religious books for children.

Summer family retreats at Spode House, the Dominican center in Stratfordshire, introduced Haughton to the land movement, which these Dominicans had fostered since the 1930s, long before many others became concerned about ecological issues. Just as she had been attracted to some of the early Catholic lay community movements, she was drawn to the land movement. Its distributist doctrines of collaboration, decentralization, environmental concern, and simplicity of lifestyle appealed to her. They also influenced her developing sense of church. In a 1969 book she comments on her attitude at the time:

> It so happens that I am, as far as my politics are coherent, rather far to the left. I am all for what St. Paul calls the overturning of the established order, and a system of government that would give something approaching real equality and freedom. I am revolted to the point of nausea by class and racial prejudice and all the other horrible things that are bred from fear and ignorance, including clerical caste consciousness.[19]

Throughout her life, Haughton's sociopolitical convictions have remained a foundation of her action on behalf of the victimized and oppressed members of society.

---

19. Rosemary Haughton, *The Changing Church* (London: Chapman, 1969), 38-39.

As her family grew, Haughton continued to read avidly, particularly in the area of theology. The works of authors from the era of the Second Vatican Council, especially Karl Rahner and Edward Schillebeeckx, led her to question the established understanding, standards, and ideals that had marked Catholicism at the time of her conversion. At the same time, she found hope and inspiration in Thomas Merton, the Trappist monk whose works she had read eagerly since she was a teenager:

> He symbolized for me through many years the unat-
> tainable good that always eluded me. He remained the
> sign and guarantee of the still, vivid, and incorruptible
> heart in a religion that had all too many obviously
> deathly and trivial aspects.[20]

Merton remained a favorite of Haughton's. As his horizons expanded and his social consciousness developed, she found in his later works both a source for her own reflections and an affirmation of them.

During the Second Vatican Council, Haughton found that she needed to write in order to think through new ideas. Out of these essentially personal reflections came a series of articles for adults which examined contemporary Catholic issues in light of the conciliar documents. Eventually, these articles led to books, lectures, BBC radio and television appearances, and invitations for lecture tours, first in the United States and later in Canada and Australia.[21]

---

20. Rosemary Haughton, "Bridge between Two Cultures," *Catholic World* 209 (May 1969): 53.

21. Haughton's first lecture tour in the United States, in 1965, came about at the suggestion of Mary Reed Newland, a "pen-friend" of hers. Newland introduced Haughton to Margaret Kelley, her own lecture agent, who became a life-long friend to Haughton. Haughton recalls she told Kelley, "Treat me like a parcel and mail me around!"

During a lecture tour in the United States in October 1967, Haughton had the opportunity to meet Thomas Merton at the Abbey of Gethsemani, near Louisville, Kentucky. At the time, she was almost seven months pregnant with her tenth child. The brief afternoon spent talking over a picnic lunch, looking at his photographs, and discussing Christian community and the cultural task of Christianity had a lasting influence on Haughton. She was touched by "his *complete* humanness, one that did not reject secular culture, or bow down to it, but made it fully human by the presence of Christ."[22]

Because Merton both typified his European cultural background and exhibited the vitality of America, Haughton saw in him a real bridge between the European and United States cultures. For her, his genuine Christianity created this bridge.

> It was the depth and sensitivity he had acquired through contemplation, through liturgy and the discipline of theology, sifting motives, valuing human life by the standard of the kingdom that brought two cultures together and made them something unique, new, and exciting.[23]

Haughton immediately recognized the importance of this insight for her, "So, for the first time, I, a European, was given a sense of the real value of the elusive thing called

---

22. Haughton, "Bridge between Two Cultures," 54. Merton's reaction to Haughton is recorded by John Howard Griffin in *Follow the Ecstasy: Thomas Merton, the Hermitage Years, 1965-1968* (Fort Worth: JHG Editions/Latitude Press, 1983), 17: "She impressed Fr. Louis [Merton] as a quiet and intelligent lady, concerned about true contemplative life. She impressed him also as being the first theologian he had ever met who was six months pregnant. He photographed her in a long black cloak with her hair blowing in the wind as she sat on the concrete dam of Dom Frederick's Lake."

23. Haughton, "Bridge between Two Cultures," 54.

America, *from inside,* as I experienced it in one man's mind." Years later, on several occasions, Haughton acknowledged how Merton's vision of future monastic communities as small groups of people called to prayer, shared living, and being the heart of a wider Christian community, influenced her own attempts at family-based communities.

A simplicity of life prevailed at home as Haughton grappled with how Jesus' teaching on poverty applied to lay people, especially married ones with children. The solution seemed to lie in the early Christians' model of holding things in common. Within their family life, this included spending time together. Since each family member played a musical instrument, they enjoyed their own entertainment of sing-alongs, family concerts, and plays. Special occasions naturally became family events. For example, Elizabeth made her First Communion during Sue's wedding Mass, and Mark was an altar server. Rosemary iced the wedding cake, which Algy had made, and arranged all the bouquets.

The growing Haughton family eventually included seven boys and three girls plus two legal foster children and several unofficial foster children. In addition, their door was always open for others in need of support or comfort. In comments made to an interviewer in 1970 when they were eighteen, the older twins, Barney and Benet, provide a picture of the Haughtons' blend of family loyalty and social consciousness:

> "When the village children were all eager to use [the swimming pool], Mummy charged a penny a time and gave the money to charitable organizations, such as Oxfam, which feeds the hungry," Benet said. "We often call our home 'The Haughton Hotel' since friends so often ring up and want a bed for the night," Barney added. "All year round, too. Mummy is catering for more than just the family. It's a village of large families, but ours is still the largest."[24]

Another example of the Haughtons' regular outreach to others is found in their participation in a Christmas 1968 benefit performance of a short children's opera, Benjamin Britten's *The Little Sweep*, put on by the children of the village to raise funds for homeless families.

Despite the apparent togetherness of the family during these years, Rosemary Haughton's personal experience was far from a blissful ideal of Christian marriage and family. In a later essay, she reveals some of the inner struggles she endured at the time. She describes an extended period of disillusionment and "dismal, obstinate clinging on to shreds of idealism and hope." Her natural persistence coupled with the family momentum of hospitality and practical Christianity carried her through this dark and lonely period. Some of the lessons from half-understood and nearly forgotten books from her teens also sustained her:

> Why should I pretend? I asked myself. I shan't be the first or the last who has discovered that Christianity, however beautiful, is not real after all. I've struggled and tried and carried on, and it has let me down. But another voice, instructed by the great masters, replied firmly, "If there *is* any truth in all that you have believed, you won't rediscover it by cutting the wires."[25]

Strengthened by this insight, Haughton carried on with the usual routine of going to Mass and teaching the children, even though it was more depressing and difficult than ever to balance writing as a Catholic for Catholics, without committing herself to beliefs in which she now found little meaning. In the end, perseverance prevailed and she experienced a personal breakthrough. From these dark times,

---

24. Kathleen Britten, "Rosemary Haughton at Home," *Way-Catholic Viewpoint* 26, no. 3 (April 1970): 29.

25. Haughton, "Avoiding Vanity Fair," 162-3.

Rosemary emerged into a new period of light, one far brighter than she had known before.

Haughton credits this victory over inner darkness to a blind commitment to prayer encouraged by a friend who told her: "Pray! If you can do no more – yell at God, scream at him in anger and pain – but pray!" Another friend, a nun, she recalls, "pushed me 'over the edge' and I found the simplest prayer, the one that is really the only possible kind for people who must be always on the run – that odd, unpredictable 'unknowing' of contemplation." At forty-six Haughton found that she had learned, at last, to stop running for running's sake. This experience freed her to enter into a new phase of her life, the beginnings of which were already actually forming.

Around 1970, the Haughtons and several of their older children had considered the idea of running a summer camp for troubled youngsters. Although they eventually abandoned this project as impractical, it sowed the seeds for another idea, the concept of a full-time family based community which would reach out to troubled young people

Family-Based Christian Community: Lothlorien Years (1973-1980)

During their years with the students' theater, the Haughtons had discovered the value to young people of working on a large undertaking, with each person filling a special role. As the idea for a new community grew, they wanted to do something that would be an expansion of their family experience. They searched for a way to share their convictions about Christian values, education, and a less wasteful lifestyle. As Haughton recalls, they envisioned something that could be a good, realistic life, a decent future for the new generation, beyond the sick dreams of processed affluence; a way to use the earth and its life respectfully, efficiently, and gratefully to increase fertility and reduce waste. As Christians, we were reaching out for something closer to the gospel ideal, something less "worldly," to use the traditional phrase.[26]

Besides making concrete their concern for troubled individuals, the community project was also an expression of the Haughtons' continued dissatisfaction with the educational system and their uneasiness with prevailing consumer-oriented values.

It isn't education, it's processing, to keep a consumer society ticking over, either as consumers of things they don't need or as producers of goods they get no good from. . . . Couldn't our family home be made big enough, in numbers and space, to create a real community, one in which others could join for a while and share the life and the work, study, talk, grow, and learn?[27]

At the same time, like many of their generation, the older children were searching for new patterns of family and lifestyle. Ultimately, all of these factors converged. After pondering the matter for two years, the family decided to take a leap in faith and go ahead with the project. As Haughton notes, "It was drastic, but it was practical."

So, in the fall of 1973, after twenty years in Yorkshire, the extended family group embarked on a faith-led project called Lothlorien, an experiment in community living on nine acres in rural southwest Scotland, near Dumfries.

---

26. Rosemary Haughton, "Lothlorien: Where I Have to Be," *Sign* 56, no. 5 (February 1977): 28.

27. Rosemary Haughton, "Lothlorien," *Sign* 53, no. 5 (Feb. 1974): 13.

Named by previous owners after the Elves' woodland home in Tolkien's *Lord of the Rings,* Lothlorien represented a complete break with a way of life that had included comparative financial security, occupational stability, a comfortable home and a bountiful garden. Just as Tolkien's Elves' refuge was not an escape, so this community experiment became to the Haughtons a "stronghold of sanity and hope in a world under threat of death and worse." It was intended to be a place where people could come for a temporary period of healing and friendship. Only many years later did Haughton publicly acknowledge an additional catalyst for the experiment in community was concern for her husband's alcohol-related problems and his need for emotional healing after years of struggling with what he considered a disastrous academic value system.[28]

When the proceeds from the sale of the family home in Yorkshire proved insufficient to purchase land with a house, they invested in land and planned to build their own house. The migration north began in January 1974 when the four older Haughton sons and one new daughter-in-law, Pauline, moved onto the property in trailers. Soon they began to plant a garden and develop a small farm. When two more sons and the wife and baby of one joined the pioneers in the spring, the group began to dig foundations for the house. Rosemary, Algy, and the younger children remained in Yorkshire until July 1974, living in a trailer home while he served out his year's notice at Ampleforth. Pauline's elderly mother joined them in the summer as grandmother to the community, just in time for the arrival of Pauline and Nick's first baby.

While "The House" slowly took shape, the extended family community lived in a motley group of trailers, with

---

28. Rosemary Haughton, *Song in a Strange Land* (Springfield, Ill.: Templegate, 1990), 48.

disused army huts donated by Cistercian monks serving as workshops and storage places. The builders worked on the foundations while others cleared the fields of rocks and put in hedges to prepare for a larger kitchen garden. Pigs dug out rough roots and fertilized the soil. Old friends came and brought their friends along and all contributed their skills to the building or the gardening tasks. A huge makeshift ridge tent served as the dining room for the summer visitors. In the evenings, everyone gathered around the campfire to relax or enjoy community sing-alongs.

After surviving the first winter in such cramped conditions, the group rejoiced when the first beam was laid in spring 1975. At Easter, they celebrated an adaptation of the Passover. Emma, the youngest Haughton, asked the ritual question of her father, "Why is this night different from all other nights?" Retelling the ancient story of the Hebrews' entry into a new land became an unforgettable experience that bound the family together in determination and hope.

Gradually, the community cleared more garden space, planted field crops and an orchard, and harvested the hay. At every turn, new skills had to be learned – rearing calves, milking cows, making cheese, butchering meat, and using herbs. The community survived financially on Haughton's writing and lecture fees and the men's earnings from occasional forestry jobs. The group maintained its spiritual energy through various community gatherings and rituals. Those who felt inclined met for periods of meditation in the early morning. Study groups explored the basis of Lothlorien ideals. Because they believed that true celebration is a religious act, happy times were celebrated with enthusiasm – Christmas, birthdays, and the appearance of visitors.

By February 1977, the house was nearly finished, although it had been partially occupied for two years. In that time, three babies had been born. Nick, Pauline, and their little ones had moved to Leeds, where he took a job in social work. Six more adults and two children had joined the group. During this time of growth and transformation, the community established the Lothlorien Trust to carry out its aims of education, proper care of the land, and hospitality, particularly for those in need. The household extended its hand most especially to the elderly, the disturbed, and disoriented young people. In time, they focused on the needs of the mentally ill. In an article on Lothlorien, Haughton remarks, "It is a good place, a place for hoping, in a world that needs hope."

Lothlorien was a mixed, ecumenical, multi-generational community attempting to live in harmony with the earth. It reminded Haughton of her conversation with Merton and his vision of future Christian communities as loose-knit associations gathered around a more permanent core. In retrospect she writes, "That chaotic but rewarding experience reinforced the sense of the land as the literal basis of human life and community, land as the source of wealth and health, land as God's gift, not as a commodity to be exploited."[29] Haughton's belief in the significance of the land would later also play a major part in her future community-building venture in the United States.

Although Haughton had envisioned Lothlorien as the fulfillment of her dreams of a family-based Christian community, it was not to be so. New theological insights as well as some personal difficulties marked these years. Together they led first to further developments in her consciousness and ultimately to the next stage of her life journey. As the seventies drew to a close, Haughton experienced an inner restlessness and an undefinable sense of impending change. At the same time, a series of birth dreams hinted at a new beginning, at some new form of life emerging. Lothlorien had in many ways become Haughton's picture of Christian

---

29. Haughton, "Re-Discovering Church," 5.

community life, and so her decision to leave formed gradually and painfully.

During this period, the Vatican II understanding of
church as the People of God influenced Haughton's theological thinking. The new developments appealed to her
because she recognized in them a rediscovery of the earliest
Christian tradition of church. During her lecture tours, her
experiences of the grassroots Catholic Church in the United
States provided a living example that confirmed her changing
notion of church. Both of these forces gradually directed
her interest toward the growing number of small Christian
communities in the United States. In addition, by the mid-
1970s Haughton realized that her reading of Christian feminist authors had confirmed her own previously inarticulate
feelings of anger and protest toward the role and treatment
of women in society. She discovered she had become a
feminist in terms of her critical analysis of theology and the
Church. This shift proved to be crucial for her own future.

New Beginnings: Wellspring Community (1980-)

A decisive moment for Haughton came in 1979 when she
made a long visit to be with her sister Virginia in the difficult
time following their father's death. Her stay in Surrey was
a kind of home-coming because Virginia lived in the sixteenth-century house which their parents had bought after
the war. Since their mother's death in 1969, Virginia had
lived there, keeping house for her father and raising her
sister Elizabeth's two little girls after their mother's untimely
death. Although Rosemary had never lived in the house,
except for vacations, it was full of the furniture that meant
home to her, and she loved it.

Away from Lothlorien, Haughton found space and quiet
to reflect on her own situation. It had been becoming

increasingly clear to her for some time that she felt she no longer fitted or was wanted at Lothlorien. This, though painful, was part of the process that would eventually result in separation. In Surrey she was able to think about a number of issues and to recognize in the course of events what she felt to be a call to work more directly with the poor. In particular, Haughton thought that she needed to be involved with the small Christian communities developing in the United States. Her major theological work, *The Passionate God*, which was written at Virginia's house, originated in her struggle to deal with a number of painful issues and to articulate her theological reflection at the time.

In July 1979, Haughton began to share her emerging vision. She sent a photocopied hand-written letter to a small number of friends, whom she addressed as "friends and companions on the way." In this letter she explained her hope to encourage new expressions of church. She wrote, "I have finally come to realise that the Lord is asking me to commit myself entirely to this mission. . . . And because of the nature of the work and of the times it is clear that I cannot do it as a profession or a 'career' but only as a response to God's calling, as completely as I can."[30]

In the fall of 1979, during this period of searching, Haughton began another lecture tour in the United States. By now she had accepted what she felt was a clear call to a different way of life but had no conscious sense of what its direction would be. Years later, she observed, "In fact I had 'decided', and only needed to find adequate religious language and religious imagination to provide a convincing support and context for what was deeply and simply a need

---

30. I discovered this letter in the archives of the Lonergan Research Institute in Toronto in Bernard Lonergan's file on Rosemary Haughton. I am indebted to Fr. Fred Crowe, S.J., for bringing this material to my attention.

for spiritual/personal survival."[31] Once again, various circumstances would converge to suggest the resolution of her questions.

While Haughton was leading a day of reflection for married couples at a parish in Peabody, near Boston, she was introduced to a parish scripture study group, some of whose members were considering direct involvement in social ministry. The vision of the group appealed to Haughton and she made plans to visit them again the following January.

Hoping to reach a decision about her future direction, Haughton made a thirty-day retreat at the Jesuit retreat house in Guelph, near Toronto, Canada. This experience provided her with the religious language she needed to confirm the plans her imagination had already set in motion. Evaluating the retreat in hindsight, Haughton recognizes the limitations of her discernment even while acknowledging the action of the Spirit:

> At the time it was a marvelous experience, and indeed it brought to the surface many memories and feelings which I was able to accept and integrate into my life in a new way. But it was dangerously self-validating. It reinforced what I wanted to reinforce and gave the power and authority of a religious insight to the fantasies I needed in order to continue in the path I had chosen. It also gave a specious conviction of absoluteness to the lifestyle I wanted and needed at the time.[32]

In the same recollection Haughton emphasizes the power of imagination. Even though it is limited by the scope of the images it uses, imagination remains the essential tool of liberation. Vocation, she asserts, is not devalued by the

---

31. Haughton, *Song in a Strange Land*, 49.
32. Ibid., 50.

strong psychological roots of a religious calling. Rather, it expresses "the deep need to reach for a way of life in which a person can find herself, which is also to find the true God." As her experience later proved, the vision inspired by imagining something different often has to be modified when it encounters reality.

This transition in Haughton's life did not occur without long, drawn-out and difficult discussions with her family. With the exception of Emma, the children were adults by now. Some of them, however, did not relish the idea of their mother living for most of the year in the United States. While Algy believed that his personal call was to remain with Lothlorien, Rosemary was resolved to work with the emerging Christian communities in the United States and to develop a missionary movement aimed at the inner city and rural American poor.

When the family eventually gave Rosemary their support to test her vision, she and Algy set out on their separate ways amicably. In addition to their increasingly different senses of personal calling, they recognized an additional factor in their decision. This was the repeated but unsuccessful attempts they had made to resolve Algy's alcohol-related problems.

A more fundamental reason for their parting, which was not openly mentioned at the time, was Algy's realization that he needed to acknowledge the fact of his own homosexuality. Like many people of their generation, Rosemary and Algy had both believed and hoped that this could be somehow ignored or overcome. Rosemary explains that this very personal issue was not openly discussed even then, but today, at a much later date, both Rosemary and Algy are able simply to name the fact, which in spite of many hard years and experiences did not contradict the good memories and achievements of their marriage.[33] They did not divorce, and continue to visit each other and share family occasions and celebrations. On one occasion, responding to assumptions that she and her husband had legally separated, Rosemary remarked, "The really close friends understood. Somebody, I think it was C. S. Lewis, talked about people facing ahead side-by-side rather than looking into each other's eyes. Ours has always been that kind of marriage."[34]

After a difficult Christmas at Lothlorien, Haughton returned to the parish in Peabody in early 1980. She led retreats and workshops and participated in the scripture group. Whenever she could, she studied intensely about small Christian communities, the call to simplicity of life, and commitment to the poor. This way of dealing with her need for freedom and growth in response to her personal struggles was not without its flaws. However, in hindsight she concludes that it was good and necessary.

Haughton believed that through her experience at Lothlorien she had learned what it meant to live with people in need. She also felt that this background, combined with her exposure to the American scene during her frequent visits, gave her a sense of what could be done on the local-church level. In actual fact, as she remarked in an interview later: "I was rather confused. In my usual fashion I was trying to rationalise things and explain it all neatly. But it couldn't be explained neatly, I simply had a strong sense of vocation toward being part of a 'new growth' community or movement."[35]

Haughton's first attempt to embody what she believed to be her new calling involved meeting with small church groups across the United States in early 1980. In these

---

33. I am deeply grateful to Rosemary Haughton for recently providing the material for this section of this manuscript.

34. Jones, "One Woman's Progress," 80.

35. Ibid.

meetings she encouraged the participants to shift their concept of church from a purely parish focus to a broader vision of Christian life and work. Not only did this venture proved unsuccessful, but the draining exertion it involved led to physical and emotional exhaustion on her part.

A very tired Haughton returned to Peabody realizing she had forgotten that St. Paul had settled in for months on end in the communities with which he worked! Shortly before a trip to England for Christmas 1980, she acknowledged:

> Stress and anxiety, brought on by refusing to recognize my own physical and emotional limitations, had exposed the limits of the image which had enabled me to break free. Its validity had been in its power to energize and liberate. It was not sufficiently in touch with reality to allow it to provide a whole way of life, which is what I had tried to make it do.[36]

Fortunately, at the moment when reality broke in on Haughton, the Peabody scripture group's plans offered new possibilities to her. She sensed a way to live out the essentials of her dream in the context of a group that would provide the support and companionship which she needed.

At the same time that Haughton was struggling with her own issues, the import of the radical gospel message about liberation and commitment had become disturbingly clear to some members of the scripture group. After a period of restless questioning for many of them, a few members of the group decided to respond to the challenge in a practical manner. The basic idea became clear when Nancy Schwoyer, the parish religious education director, proposed a community base, a place to work and live together, to which people in need could turn.

---

36. Haughton, *Song in a Strange Land*, 59.

While they considered the details of such an undertaking, all the hope, fear, excitement, dreaming and praying of the group took flesh in the person of "Jane." This tear-stained seventeen-year-old, escaping from a situation of intolerable abuse, appeared on their doorstep in light clothing one snowy night in late 1980. Haughton recollects that "Jane's coming suddenly gave a very concrete form to the new sense of direction which was being tentatively and privately discerned."

And so by early 1981, the reality of a place of hospitality, a community and a refuge for the homeless, began to take shape. From this small beginning grew Wellspring House in nearby Gloucester, Massachusetts, an economically depressed fishing port. The Wellspring Community occupied one of the oldest houses in the United States, built in 1649, and once owned by a juror at the Salem witch trials. The community considered itself a cell of the universal church, or to use an early Christian term, a *house church*.

The story of the purchase of the Gloucester property in April 1981 and the development of Wellspring House and its various programs during the 1980s is told by Haughton in *Song in a Strange Land*. In itself the old house became a symbol of homecoming. It served as a paradigm of the whole project of trying to restore a sense of home to both the earth and its people through providing a shelter and resources for the homeless.

In 1982, Wellspring became the base from which Haughton and Nancy Schwoyer launched another project, an ecumenical lay missionary group to address the needs of the rural and inner-city poor. They envisioned this new project, "Movement for North American Mission," as a movement of friends supporting each other in their commitment to the gospel. By stressing unity built on commitment to the gospel, they hoped to bypass doctrinal barriers. People interested in joining the Movement received an intense five week orientation program prior to a two-year assignment in a depressed area.

The Movement was discontinued after three years for various reasons, including concern about the type of applicants the program appeared to draw. Orientation weekends at Wellspring had quickly revealed that many people saw service to the poor as a means to personal and spiritual fulfillment. This approach was alien to the Wellspring philosophy of working for systemic change. Haughton writes:

> We did not experience in such people any anger at injustice or abuse, nor much real understanding of what poverty does to people. Rather it seemed that "the poor" became the object of a quasi-romantic devotion which isolated its object from the rest of life and people, and in an odd way dehumanized those it claimed to serve. . . . In such people there was no sign of the energy of compassion which shows itself as appropriate anger, raising a need to understand the causes for the suffering of the poor, and to address the causes as well as the effects.[37]

At the same time, the rapid development of the Wellspring project made it necessary to set priorities and make choices about their resources. During the three years the Movement lasted, however, Haughton and Schwoyer trained and placed volunteers in inner city community groups in Chicago, Gary, and south Boston, as well as with the rural poor in Appalachia and elsewhere. During their visits with the missionaries in their placements, they learned firsthand what often really happens to poor people in affluent America.

Since dropping the idea of a home mission movement in 1984, Haughton, Schwoyer, Mary Jane Veronese and her husband Paul, who were also part of the original study group, and three others including "Jane," have continued

---

37. Ibid., 93.

serving as the core-community of Wellspring House. Many volunteers have assisted in all the new projects by joining in the work for short or long periods. As the scope of Wellspring's outreach has grown, an increasingly diverse paid staff has handled the routine details. At every level, Wellspring House has been a team effort.

Underlying the Wellspring venture was a fundamental trust that something different is possible when people dare to imagine change. Haughton remembers:

> The touchstone of the vision which fired our imagination was the gospel proclamation of a transformed human and earthly community in touch with the life of God as its own life, and open to the responsibility and opportunity that goes with that awareness.[38]

One dimension of this responsibility, one that was central to Wellspring's vision, involved viewing the land as God's land. From this perspective, they understand the land to be the basis for liberty and justice.

Through their work with homeless people, especially women and children, it soon became clear to Haughton and the others that homelessness was essentially a form of exile. It was separation from all that makes earth home for people – a dwelling, family, adequate food, community support, and meaningful work. They quickly linked this insight to the rising phenomenon of the feminization of poverty. Haughton came to understand Wellspring's relationship – both practical and metaphoric – to the exile endured by impoverished women. But in it she also saw hope that return from exile is possible for all people. In its own way, each element of the Wellspring program fit Haughton's ongoing interests in the meaning of life, the role of Christianity in

---

38. Ibid., 75.

society, and concern for marginated persons and for the earth itself.

The evolving story of Wellspring is one of a fragile hope that has grown steadily over the years. While it began as low-profile attempt to live Christian community in a house open to those in need, it has become a widely respected ecumenical and ecologically conscious program of sheltering, education, transitional housing, and economic development. Today, Wellspring responds to the challenges of homelessness in two ways. Directly, the Wellspring House Inc. (the original non-profit corporation) community extends shelter to families in need. The Wellspring Community Land Trust of Cape Ann, the second and independent corporation with its own board and staff, works to provide affordable homes and low-rent apartments. Through support groups, retreats, and workshops, Wellspring House offers educational opportunities to present and former guests and to other women and men struggling with poverty. In 1992, Wellspring obtained a small grant to create a public community garden on unused Wellspring acreage, where, with professional advice and Wellspring support, local families are able to grow healthy food economically. In 1995, Wellspring House completed a fundraising drive to build the Veronese Community Education Resource Center. Named in honor of two of Wellspring's founding members, Mary Jane and Paul Veronese, the center provides educational programs which are rooted in the experience, talents, and needs of the local Cape Ann community. It also houses the Cape Ann Food Pantry and a free-meal program for those in need. One of the latest ventures is an economic development program, Working Capital, which provides loans, networking and business assistance to the self-employed.[39]

---

39. Wellspring House, "Newsletter," July 1995.

A Board of Directors oversees the various dimensions of Wellspring. A network of staff, interns, and volunteers facilitate the programs. To support the vision, the development office raises funds from a variety of sources, including State grants and donations from local and faraway friends. Wellspring staff constantly work to develop new programs for homeless people and others in need. Careful ongoing social analysis keeps Wellspring abreast of shifting social realities. At the heart of it all, however, remain the needy, the homeless, and the victimized, whom the Wellspring community consider to be treated as aliens in their own country.

Life at Wellspring House itself, which is also the emergency family shelter, balances staff and residents' daily work and regular household routine with times of celebration and ritual. Each resident has a personal helper to assist her deal with a multitude of concerns, including court hearings, medical and agency appointments, education, budgeting, and children's needs. The rhythm of community routine grounds the often hectic days and encourages friendship and mutual support.

Mealtime prayer and an ecumenical Sunday service enable the participants to return to the well of their own faith and resources. A typical Sunday service draws upon Scripture and is prepared in turn by members of the community. More ritualized celebrations for special Christian feast days and events in the lives of the community afford extra opportunities for expressing gratitude and hope as well as suffering and uncertainty.

The story of Wellspring has both an outer and an inner dynamic. On the external level, the project has responded over the years to over three hundred families, providing them with the resources and skills necessary to take control of their lives. In the process, an inner dynamic has raised many more people's consciousness about homelessness, affordable housing, and welfare programs. The Wellspring experience has forced them to face the systemic roots of poverty and environmental crises and to consider questions without conventional answers. As Haughton notes:

> This is doing what people of faith have always had to do, trying to make sense of belief, vocation, salvation, sin, and all the other religious issues – in terms of their own time and place, their own fears and prejudices and learned responses. It is perhaps a theology of women in our society, in our land – or rather, as we discovered, of women in exile from the land.[40]

Since 1981, the Wellspring experience has formed the primary basis for Haughton's continuing reflection. The influence of Wellspring on her more recent writing is evident in the recurring themes of women's issues and the biblical paradigm of exile and homecoming. In one sense, Haughton's quest for meaning has become focused within a particular segment of society. In a wider sense, however, she has embraced all of humanity and has distilled a deeper richness from her lifetime experiences. At seventy years of age, Haughton says she remains at Wellspring because it is a way of life that makes sense to her. In a recent letter she remarked, "I think I am discovering a more Amish-like attitude to life, doing things as they come – including a lot of work in the garden and yard, growing *lots* of flowers as well as vegetables." These days, she takes more time for her own writing and intellectual exploring.

In the midst of her many activities, Haughton's family remains the most important element in her life. She keeps in close contact with them through letters, telephone calls, and annual extended visits. She is particularly eager to return

40. Ibid., 15-16.

to England for special events such as weddings and for Algy's seventieth birthday celebration in January 1993. When they can afford the journey, family members and their children occasionally spend vacation time at Wellspring.

Haughton finds that she has a very close and very different relationship with each of her children. Today, her expanding family circle includes twenty-six grandchildren and a first great-grandchild. In addition, it embraces her sister Elizabeth's two daughters and their children and Haughton's surviving sister, Virginia. She feels that her relationship with Virginia is special because they share memories no one else has. Also, Rosemary can tell Virginia about the early years that she does not remember.

Conclusion

Over the years Rosemary Haughton has developed gradually but steadily as a contemporary laywoman, able to integrate her Christianity with her everyday experience and to critique social institutions, both civil and ecclesiastical. At each stage of her life, Haughton has pursued a deeper meaning of the "something important" that she first glimpsed as a small child. She has maintained the strong values and the Christian attitudes that she formed early in life.

Haughton has striven to respond to challenges with integrity and with confidence in the message of Jesus and in the continuing power of God's Spirit at work in the world. She has used theological reflection to clarify for herself and for others the meaning of the gospel for people living at the end of the twentieth century. Although her life has in many ways been remarkable, Haughton has matured primarily through the ordinary stuff of life. Both her thought and her example offer insights into a contemporary Christian spirituality that finds hope and meaning in the midst of modern life and its uncertainties. The next chapter focuses specifically on her theology.

Chapter Three

Proclaiming the Passionate God: Haughton's Theology

> *[Theology is] the poetic evocation of human events in such a way as to make clear their divine significance. So if I say that God is passionate, and that this gives us the key to the whole nature of reality, I am making a theological statement which is strictly poetic. The poetry of passionate love is the accurate language of theology.*
>
> – Rosemary Haughton, *The Passionate God*[1]

Tutored primarily in the school of experience and personal study, Rosemary Haughton does not claim to be a systematic theologian or a scripture scholar. These are not her gifts or professional training. She came to theology from another direction, from a personal need to make sense of her own experience. She sees herself as an educated woman, although not an academic, who has tried to interpret the Christian tradition through a form of expression understandable to people today. To her surprise, in the process she discovered that what was unfolding was theology.

Aware of her limitations, Haughton recognizes that she speaks about Christian life from an Anglo-European and North American background, particularly from within the Roman Catholic experience in Britain and the United States.

---

1.   Rosemary Haughton, *The Passionate God* (Mahwah, NJ: Paulist Press, 1981), 14.

At the same time, in continuity with Julian of Norwich and other women before her, she claims the right to speak out from a particular experience, in a particular time and place, about Christians' relationship with God, with the hope that her words will not be limited to her own time and place.[2]

Haughton's Understanding of Theology

When Haughton speaks of theology, she means more than an academic discipline. She includes other serious and deliberate attempts to understand the relationship between God and human beings, the deepest meaning of life, wherever this relationship takes place. She believes that precisely because theology is concerned with the total human situation, it is important to get away from the notion of theology as only ready-made principles or patterns to which experience must be shaped and to recognize it also as a discovery of the ways of the living God in our midst.

Haughton believes that the theological task is to try to articulate the complexities of God's love affair with human minds, bodies, and spirits – all of these, and all together. Theology is successful in this task to the degree that its

---

2. Haughton's reflections about human life and theology permeate her writings. Several books provide more comprehensive presentations of her thought. *On Trying to Be Human* (1966) and *Transformation of Man* (1967) in particular present the basic elements of Haughton's early writing on human existence. In *The Changing Church* (1969) she presents her vision for a renewed church. The basic elements of her theological method are found in *Theology of Experience* (1972). *The Catholic Thing* (1980) contains insightful reflections on the meaning of church as does *There is Hope for a Tree: A Study Paper on the Emerging Church* (1981). Later developments in her theological thought, as well as a synthesis of much of her earlier writings on the meaning of human existence, are in *The Passionate God* (1981). Many of the longer essays written since 1980 include her more recent thought on specific contemporary issues.

formulations accomplish a recognizable expression of the human experience of the divine. In practice, therefore, the threefold work of the theologian is to reflect lucidly on the Christian consciousness gained from the experience of God's action in human history, to communicate this reflection to others in an understandable way, and to interpret the tradition through the study of doctrines developed in earlier periods of Christian experience.

Haughton insists that good theology cannot be conducted in an intellectual laboratory divorced from daily experience.[3] Rather, the theological process has to take place in the undefinable but real gap between strong feeling about human issues and choosing a committed Christian response to events. Ultimately, in Haughton's perception, theology is the revelation of Wisdom, by which she means the apprehension of God throughout human experience "in one historical yet eternal point, physical and spiritual and personal and cosmic."[4]

Haughton also emphasizes that since human experience is not limited to one person or group, good theology cannot be done in isolation, but must be the work of the whole Church. Also, because the Church is rooted in history, theology at any given time can describe only how people view the world and the divine-human relationship in that era. Consequently, she argues, each person is called to become sensitive to God's work in his or her own time and to proclaim it. Although many people do not recognize the fact, everyone has a theological work to do, because every

---

3. In *The Catholic Thing*, 16, Haughton suggests that barren, overrational theology historically has often been at the root of the abusive use of religion.

4. Haughton, *The Passionate God*, 4. Haughton uses the term *wisdom* in several senses in different contexts to refer to God's Spirit, to Jesus as incarnate Wisdom, to the nurturing quality of God, or to a profound understanding of God's presence in human life.

practical decision implies theological assumptions and forms part of the tradition from which others will later draw for their decisions.

Haughton is convinced that theology on all levels has an important role in the Church for at least three reasons. First, whenever Christian theology presents a meaningful explanation of the divine-human relationship, people discover the wisdom of Christianity, the full meaning of life, because it rings true with their experience. On the other hand, people frequently reject the gospel due to inadequate or incomprehensible theology. When theology runs dry and theological concepts become hollow, it can no longer truly be called theology because it does not communicate people's experience of God, who is Love. It has become "a sounding brass and a tinkling cymbal."[5]

Second, theology is important for the Church because it is formative. Through the understanding of life which it presents, theology shapes people's thinking and action in response to their experiences. In this way, good theology prepares them for and leads them toward true inner conversion. In turn, the formative aspect of theology is developed by being more fully understood through experience in real situations.

Third, effective theology sharpens people's understanding of the nature of the Church and its mission in the world. It illuminates the role of the Christian community as the extension of Jesus' mission in the world. Less developed theology, Haughton believes, often leads to privatized re-

---

5. In *The Catholic Thing,* Haughton relates her personal sadness over her mother's disenchantment with Catholicism not many years after her conversion because of its "preoccupation with the rules, the intolerance and narrowness," and over the departure, following the publication of *Humanae Vitae* in 1968, of Charles Davis, once considered one of the foremost English-speaking Roman Catholic theologians.

ligion and does not encourage people to get involved in issues of the day and to take appropriate action for justice and human rights.

An important aspect of Haughton's concept of theology is her insight that in its interpretation of the divine-human relationship, theology itself is a language, a special, exacting language capable of unfolding the mysteries of Christian faith and life. She uses the term *language* in this context in the fullest sense of not only words but also gesture and the whole range of symbolic communication. She includes the total cultural message conveyed by a particular milieu, for instance, the language of the Church or the language of contemporary culture.

Haughton draws a parallel between theology and poetry because the languages of both poetry and theology are always searching for words to convey a truth that is infinitely precise yet incapable of complete articulation. In *The Passionate God*, she writes:

> Poetry is not "illustration" of prose by adding imagery; it is rather the most accurate way in which some inkling of an incommunicable experience can be communicated, and theology is exactly that also. It is in the struggle to articulate truthfully that the words become capable of actually communicating truth, for if they are the right words they take to themselves some of the power of the experience and break through into the mind that listens, creating a communion of experience.[6]

In a similar fashion, theology strains to find words to express what is often inexpressible. In Haughton's words,

> [Theology is] the poetic evocation of human events in such a way as to make clear their divine significance.

---

6. Haughton, *The Passionate God*, 6.

> So if I say that God is passionate, and that this gives us the key to the whole nature of reality, I am making a theological statement which is strictly poetic. The poetry of passionate love is the accurate language of theology.[7]

Consequently, theologians must be adept at the use of image and symbol, the poetic use of language, in order to communicate the deepest meaning of our relationship with God.

Haughton has spent thirty-five years exploring the meaning of this interrelationship between experience and theology and trying to explain it to others. Her conclusion is that:

> Theology is not a system invented by religious people and then applied to existing human concerns. It is simply a reflection, in the light of faith, on what actually happens to people – to individual people, and to groups and nations and cultures. Theology is the attempt to find more or less adequate and comprehensible ways of conveying what we perceive of human events as the action of God towards human beings, and the response of human beings to God.[8]

Haughton's perspective on theology is grounded in her practical approach to the mysteries of life and faith. As the next section indicates, her theological method is influenced by her perception of the nature and task of theology.

---

7. Ibid., 14. Haughton's use of the language of medieval romance literature, particularly of the term *passion*, is discussed in a later section of this chapter. At this point, it suffices to note that she uses "passion" to refer to an experience involving "the drive of a powerful emotion towards the knowledge, and in some sense, possession, of an object outside oneself."

8. Haughton, *The Catholic Thing*, 228.

Haughton's "Theology of Experience"

Haughton uses a theological approach that she calls "theology of experience." She uses "experience" to name not simply a happening or an emotional uplift but the entire horizontal, experiential dimension of life as perceived by an individual or group of people in their daily activities. By "theology of experience" Haughton means careful reflection, enlightened by faith, on God's ways with humankind as perceived in experience. In her own words,

> The "theology of experience" . . . means, essentially, a realization that a healthy and living theology must grow out of actual experience and cannot thrive if each generation of theologians busies itself with separating yet more strands of speculation from the yarn spun by the previous one. The fact is that *all* good theology is, and always has been, a theology of experience. To explore the idea now is to be thoroughly traditional in the proper and necessary sense, and therefore to break new ground.[9]

This new ground is the ongoing experience of God at work in human lives, an experience that varies according to particular eras, cultures, and philosophies, and drives people continually to find new ways to describe God's action in their midst.

---

9. Haughton, *Theology of Experience*, 9. Her insistence that relevatory experience must be consciously received but need not be "religious" reflects the shift of emphasis in contemporary theology from first principles to experience. Dermot Lane, in *The Experience of God: An Invitation to Do Theology* (New York: Paulist, 1985), provides a concise introduction to a contemporary understanding of the relationship between experience and theology. See also the entry "Experience," *Dictionary of Theology*, new rev. ed. (1985), ed. K. Rahner and H. Vorgrimler.

Haughton believes the renewed emphasis on experience in contemporary theology is important because in the past abstract concepts have often replaced experience as the basis of theological discussion. In her work, Haughton draws not only on her own experience but also on a wide range of biographical, psychological, and historical accounts of human experience, and literary images and themes. In *Theology of Experience*, Haughton explains her approach in detail. Both to support her method and to demonstrate how it functions, she presents a number of examples from scripture and Christian theology that illustrate how our ancestors in faith drew their theology from their understanding of God's action in their lives.[10] First, she recalls how the Hebrew people, shaken by exile and the destruction of their nation, were able through the teaching of the Isaiah to recognize God's action in Cyrus, a Gentile. Through this experience, they received the revelation that God was not an outsider but was active in their midst. Their new realization that God's plan extended beyond Israel made them rethink their notion of God's will and their role as a nation in God's plan (Is. 41-48).

Turning to Jesus' teaching, Haughton notes that because he spoke with authority, we often fail to see that he also spoke from experience about discerning the nature and will of God by observing the behavior of ordinary people. Referring to the parables about the generous father and a trapped sheep, Haughton adds, "So the lesson of God's endless forgiveness is drawn from the behaviour to be expected of an ordinary father, and God's will that the sick should be healed on the Sabbath is deduced from the practical behaviour of any sensible man who owns an animal."[11] In other words, human experience of the natural

---

10. Haughton, *Theology of Experience*, 10-16.
11. Ibid., 11-12. See Lk. 15:11-21 and Mt. 12:11-12.

impulse to be caring and helpful indicates something about God and about our own nature as God's creatures.

In a third scriptural example of theology of experience, Haughton refers to Paul's admonition to the Galatians about their allowing the Judaizers to persuade them that their experience of conversion and freedom in Christ was not sufficient. Paul appealed to the Galatians' personal experience and asked them to judge the matter for themselves, based on their experience and an honest answer to the question, "Was it because you practiced the Law that you received the Spirit, or because you believed what was preached to you?" (Gal. 3:1-5).

Next, taking an example from the history of Christian theology, Haughton notes that in many of his arguments St. Thomas Aquinas appealed to the experience of his readers.[12] Although today some of his interpretations, which he based on the scientific information available to him, are judged to be faulty, it is clear that Thomas regarded the reference to verifiable data essential to the development of a sound theology.

Haughton's final example of theology of experience is Karl Rahner's use of common experience to teach a theological truth. She refers to his "The Development of Dogma," in which Rahner uses the example of falling in love to explain the existence of a kind of knowledge that cannot first be expressed in formal statements but is the experiential basis from which such statements may eventually develop.[13] Haughton emphasizes that it takes a special type of aware-

---

12. Haughton specifically refers to his discussion on free will in *Summa Theologiae* I, q. 83, a. 1.

13. Karl Rahner, "The Development of Dogma," *Theological Investigations* 1, trans. Cornelius Ernst (London: Darton, Longman and Todd, 1961), 63.

ness to be able to reflect on this prior knowledge and to articulate it as the experience of grace, of God at work.

At the same time, Haughton is conscious of the need for caution in the use of experience as a basis for theology. In particular, she points to the need to discriminate between a true insight and one distorted by prejudice or wishful thinking or emotional pressure. She recognizes that before a sure discernment can be made, all the political, social, or sectarian issues must be clarified. In real life, however, time is often limited, and a judgment has to be made on the basis of reasonable certitude of how God is present in the experience.

In response to this dilemma, Haughton distinguishes two types of theology of experience: reflective and prophetic. Both styles draw on authentic experience and both have their advantages and disadvantages. The reflective style, which discerns the action of God in the long term, tends to be cautious and thorough. Over time it builds up the heritage of Christian moral sensibility as a basis for decision making. This style can also be overly hesitant and remain indecisive until the time for action has passed. On the other hand, the prophetic style, which grasps God's action in the present, is enthusiastic and forceful, responds quickly to events, and calls for obedience to God's ways. It runs the risk, however, of being confused by its own rhetoric and encouraging hostility rather than hope.

Haughton believes both types of theology of experience are necessary because they balance and correct each other. The wider, slower movements of the reflective style challenge the sometimes narrow and short-sighted vision of prophetic enthusiasm. The prophetic style encourages critical action in response to issues of justice and truth, particularly those affecting the poor.

The spirit of true theology of experience, then, is both enthusiastic and open, both appreciative and clear-sighted. But also it is very humble. . . . It is not enough to draw true conclusions from experience, we must also experience *in love*, only then shall we find the right personal balance between the demands of the present prophet and the developing tradition. Neither is sufficient without the other, either in itself, or in ourselves as we each wrestle with the theological task.[14]

In developing her theology of experience, Haughton strives to maintain this crucial balance. In practice, she favors a predominantly prophetic approach.

In her struggles to find a language through which to express her theology of experience, Haughton adopts an inductive approach. She uses narrative theology through which she allows the meaning of experience to emerge through the descriptive passages into which she draws the reader.[15] Then she begins her theological discussion.

Haughton's conviction that theological discussion need not be abstract, that there is a place for expressing theological concepts in images and language familiar to the ordinary, non-academic person, leads her to shape carefully chosen analogies and metaphors to convey the meaning of complex theological statements. Through the creative use of imagery, she suggests ways to conceptualize the power of God at work in human society and relationships. For example, in *The Catholic Thing*, Haughton uses an allegory of twin sisters, Sophia and Mother Church, to express two

---

14. Haughton, *Theology of Experience*, 30-31.

15. Haughton, *Transformation of Man*, 242. Although she does not use the phrase *narrative theology*, Haughton's use of story to draw people into reflection on experience in order to explore theological implications and to encourage transformation and action is significant because it precedes by a number of years the descriptions of narrative theology presented by noted contemporary authors, including Sallie McFague and John Shea.

necessary dimensions of the Church, the living Spirit and the structure that facilitates encounter with the Spirit. She also describes the Church in terms of a parable using the true story of York Minster, a faith vision in stone standing on the shakiest of foundations that was stabilized and restored through the combined talent and commitment of many people.

Haughton makes use of poignant incidents, dramatic or literary references, and historic occasions, to draw out the theological significance of experiences. She frequently uses the passionate language of medieval Romance literature to express the dynamics of explicitly religious conversion and the relationship between God and humanity. She also enters into theological dialogues with psychology in an effort to describe more precisely God's movement in the human spirit.

Since she joined the Wellspring House community, Haughton has incorporated more feminist analysis into her work. She usually addresses issues in contemporary U.S. culture, particularly those related to women and marginalized segments of society. She also suggests feminist and holistic reinterpretations of some traditional ascetical practices and prayer forms that no longer reflect our experience or appear to justify oppression. For example, in a 1991 Lenten series in the *National Catholic Reporter*, she addresses some traditional Lenten themes from the perspective of the effect on women's development of a spirituality designed primarily by men.

Haughton's use of scripture is one element of her methodology which has presented problems for some of her readers. At the same time, it is important to note that her approach has changed over the years from a simple meditative format to a more critical use of scripture as a reflective tool incorporating contemporary biblical scholarship.

Haughton is neither a biblical fundamentalist nor a naive interpreter of scripture. She deliberately takes a literary rather than a purely historical-critical approach to the text in an attempt to get at the experience that the text was intended to communicate and to interpret its meaning for today. So she takes scripture as a poetic description of a biblical author's perception of God's action in human history. For example, in *The Passionate God* she bases her approach to the Gospels on the assumption that the evangelists used whatever poetic categories of religious and historic imagery they needed to recount events. Haughton believes that when events could not be explained in terms that fit normal expectations, the Gospel writers used terms that created a symbolic evocation of inner experience.

Haughton's characteristic perspective on the gospels as a reliable interpretation of early Christian experience is most evident in her image of Jesus. In her analysis she attempts to reconstruct the meaning Jesus held for the first disciples. At the same time, she is clear that the gospels are a non-biographical literary form incorporating many literary styles.

Haughton's method could be termed homespun, a personal attempt to use language as a theological tool to describe reality as human beings experience it today in the light of Christian faith. Her method, however, is actually a highly complex weaving of concepts and images from history, scripture, literature, psychology, philosophy, and theology, all clothed in experiential and often poetic terms.

The Passionate God, which Haughton intended to be a synthesis of her theology, marks a major development in her use of poetic language to express theological concepts. Written in the emotionally charged context of the period of her departure from the Lothlorien community, this work burst forth in a rush of insight generated by the convergence of her questions about the meaning of the resurrection with her rediscovery of Charles Williams's writings about "the doctrine of Exchange." Although Haughton's thought has developed since she wrote *The Passionate God*, particularly with regard to feminist and social concerns, the imagery of this work is critical for an understanding of specific concepts in her anthropology, theology, and ecclesiology.

Charles Williams's model of all reality as exchange, as the continuous giving and receiving of life, provided the principal interpretive tool for Haughton's theology of the "passionate" God.[16] For terminology to explain the dynamics of the divine-human exchange, she borrowed language from the medieval French romance tradition of courtly love, with which she was familiar from Dante's *Divine Comedy*, C. S. Lewis' *The Allegory of Love*, and other works.

The language of the romance tradition appealed to Haughton because, in its ideal form, the tradition focused on the transforming power of passionate love through a disciplined yet sensitive and deeply respectful care for another. As she remarks in the introduction to *The Passionate God*:

> We can begin to make some sense of the way God loves people if we look very carefully at the way people love people, and in particular at the way of love we can refer to as "passionate" because that kind of love tells us things about how love operates which we could not otherwise know.[17]

The specific characteristics of love in the romance tradition to which Haughton refers are particularity, singularity, time-

---

16. In *The Passionate God*, Haughton explains her use of "passion" to indicate love in motion, "strong, wanting, needy, concentrated towards a very deep encounter," and also to imply "a certain helplessness, a suffering and undergoing for the sake of what is desired"(6). She believes romantic passion has the capacity for both the highest soaring and the deepest degradation (61).

17. Ibid., 6.

lessness, and painfulness. In other words, love is limited to one beloved, in a focused and timeless moment, and includes a deep longing for completeness.[18]

Haughton prefers the term "passion" to "falling in love" because she believes it better communicates the process by which people are drawn into a relationship in which they can learn to love truly. In her usage, passion does not refer to unbridled sexuality or even necessarily to sexual activity. It indicates the release of the transforming power of the deepest springs of the person, through which previously hidden elements of the personality can be expressed. In this sense, passion stands as a symbol of God's love. She also distinguishes passion from its synthetic substitutes by its outward direction and positive impact on behavior. Romantic sentimentalism, on the other hand, focuses only on the feelings produced. In response to critics who consider the modern erotic and violent image of passionate love so tarnished that it is counterproductive to use it as an image of God's love, Haughton insists on the potential of the image and on the reader's ability to interpret it appropriately.[19]

Haughton adapts Williams' model of reality as exchange for the mainspring of her description of the dynamics of human life and the divine-human relationship in terms of a constant ebb and flow of divine energy throughout creation. This energy breaks through into new levels of awareness by overcoming points of tension or obstruction. On the level of observable events, for example, exchange happens at the seashore when crashing waves break up rocks and draw the pebbles out to sea, where they eventually form barriers, which in turn reshape the flow of the tides. This "dance of the shaping earth is echoed by the dance of

18. Ibid., 54-57.
19. See Maureen Howie in a review of *The Passionate God*, in *Heythrop Journal* 24 (April 1983): 221-23.

exchanged life in the cells of living bodies," a process for which Haughton suggests only the word *love* is adequate.[20] On the human level, exchange operates principally within and through relationships.

In order to discuss this process of exchange and to express the sense of a passage from one area of experience to another through some kind of barrier or obstacle, Haughton develops the concepts of breakthrough and spheres. Breakthrough refers to a powerful impulse which manages to overcome some obstacle and pass through to a new and desired realm of experience. In her words,

> [breakthrough] can be a small personal event, such as the achievement of a shared understanding. It can be a physical event, such as the breaking of a dam, when the "need" of the water to find a way forward breaks the barriers and crashes through to the valley below. It can be a mystical experience or a scientific discovery. It can be a chicken breaking its shell or the signing of a peace treaty.[21]

Most importantly for Haughton, the experience of breakthrough makes nonsense of any concept of a division of reality into material and spiritual.

In her adaptation of Williams's model of exchange, Haughton uses the term spheres to refer to different modes of apprehending the reality which surrounds us. In contrast to Dante's use of spheres to describe the medieval cosmography of transparent concentric globes surrounding the earth, through which mortal pilgrims make their journey toward God, Haughton employs the image to convey varying dimensions and degrees of human experience encountered throughout life. As she says, spheres are "the 'layers' opened

---

20. Haughton, *The Passionate God*, 21.
21. Ibid., 18.

up by loving response to reality, and they are separated from each other by some kind of barrier, albeit a transparent one – but only transparent to eyes cleansed, as Dante's were, by the water of the river of life."[22] Haughton suggests that these responses to reality can be quite ordinary, as in the familiar transition from daily clothes, behavior, and speech to another form of dress and presentation appropriate to the celebratory sphere of a wedding or a Christmas party. Loss and grief, crisis and duty are among the many aspects of reality which also affect a person's sphere of experience.

Breakthrough affects every dimension of life. Whenever the membrane that separates spheres is crossed, even time seems to change its quality in the experience of a timeless sphere. In particular, people in love enter into even more profound and lasting changes in their sphere of experience. Haughton's interpretation of the movement between spheres combines aspects of attitude, emotion, and choice in response to life experiences, which she sees as the call of God within all reality toward the exchange of life.

By disclaiming a separation between this world and a higher world, Haughton again diverges from Dante's cosmography. She uses spheres to indicate progressively deeper levels of human consciousness rather than stages of escape from material concerns. She finds a literary example of this dimension of exchange in the children of Narnia who journey deeper and deeper towards the heart of their world following Aslan the lion, C. S. Lewis's Christ symbol.[23]

In Haughton's attempt to find language to express her theology, *exchange*, *breakthrough*, and *spheres* are related terms that provide a vocabulary to express essentially theological concepts, which she believes cannot be articulated fully in everyday language:

---

22. Ibid.
23. C. S. Lewis, *The Last Battle*.

The model of exchanged life, whose name is love, helps us to conceptualize but leaves open the way to sheer dazzlement, which is a proper reaction to the unimaginable complexity of reality. It is comparatively easy, too, to make the mental shift from "model" to verification because human love, as seen and expressed, is so clearly a matter of exchange of life, giving, upholding, renewing, responding, reaching out; a constant flow of energy which is actually the experienced nature of relationships of all kinds.[24]

Taken together, the image of reality as exchanged life and the language of passionate love provide Haughton with the descriptive tools to communicate her vision of the profound wisdom that Christianity offers.

With this introduction to Haughton's methodology and terminology in mind, we can now turn to specific elements of her theological understanding.

Haughton's Christian Anthropology

Christian anthropology studies the nature of human existence from a Christian perspective. What does it mean to be human? What is human wholeness and how does it develop? Does Christianity shed any light on the human situation? What difference does the resurrection of Jesus make? What does it mean to be genuinely Christian? How can Christians contribute to the realization of God's plan for all creation? These questions, in some form, underlie the entire body of Haughton's religious and theological work. Her thought is evident in her reflections on creation, human life, grace and sin, and human development.

---

24. Haughton, *The Passionate God*, 23.

Creation

Haughton neither speculates on the origins of creation nor deals with creation myths. She accepts creation as God's dynamic work, as a "mysterious and infinitely complex system of inter-relationships" in which every component is related to every other part because of the radical nature of exchange. She describes an ongoing process which permeates and is at work in the whole of creation even though it is at times limited and enslaved by the condition of sin in the world.

"Life" in this context means all of reality, apprehensible and inapprehensible, all that is and all that could be, and it involves thinking of everything not just as part of an infinitely complex web of inter-dependence, but as a *moving* web, a pattern of flowing, a never-ceasing in-flow and out-flow of being.[25]

Such exchange takes place in nature, for example, in rocks grinding against one another, giving and receiving matter slowly, changing and being changed.

For Haughton, the dimension of reality perceived by the human senses is not separable from immaterial reality. It is only distinguishable. Since human beings exist in space and time, exchange of life for them operates in space and time. In other words, this world is the setting of human wholeness and of humanity's relationship with God. Consequently, creation is to be recognized as holy and as God's dwelling. Every dimension of human life and experience is to be taken seriously as a reality through which God can be known better.

---

25. Ibid., 21.

Human Life

Haughton begins her search for the meaning of human life, of humanity's relationship with God, and of the role of Christianity in human development toward wholeness, with explorations of the nature of the human being. She perceives the human person as a whole body-spirit in which the mental and spiritual processes by which people grapple with the realities of their existence are continuous and organic. Haughton believes that, although limited in some respects, human beings are intrinsically free, good, and capable of development. Although the essential dimension of exchange exists in all creation, the distinctive quality of a human being is the capacity for conscious relationship and the related ability to accept or reject relationship. Humanness, therefore, means conscious freedom expressed in choice and relationship.

For Haughton, the purpose of life is to become more fully human, that is, to be more open to exchange through the responsible exercise of freedom. To be fully human is to "inherit the Kingdom," to enter ultimately into the fullness of resurrected life with Christ. What this life shall be remains a mystery and is not imaginable in terms of our present experience. To be Christian, therefore, is to be committed to walking on the edge of mystery.

Grace and Sin

Grace, in Haughton's Christian anthropology, is the eternal love of God that flows through creation, surrounding us and inviting us to transformation. From her descriptive examples, Haughton's understanding of graced life can be identified as living in harmonious relationship with the universal pattern of exchanged life. Grace is not a static image, a thing, conferred on the faithful to make them holy.

It is the loving divine energy flowing within the system of exchange of life throughout all creation.[26]

Haughton stresses that Catholic sacramental theology proclaims a world invaded and permeated by grace and called to transformation by divine love. For her, no doctrinal or ecclesial property line can be drawn around this love. Grace is universal and exists even if it is not consciously or explicitly named.

In Haughton's model of grace as God's offer of an exchange of love, sin is the refusal of this exchange, a rejection of the energy of life whose nature is to be poured out. In terms of alienation, sin is the opposite of the free and committed *amour voulu* of the romance tradition that passionately enters into the exchange of life. Where grace is essentially a relationship, sin is a block to or a violation of relationships. In terms of human behavior, sin is an individual or systemic blockage or violation of another's life, love, welfare, or liberty and reputation. Haughton contrasts sin, which she characterizes as disorder, separation, and nonsense, with love, which she identifies with peace, unity, and good sense.

Haughton describes original sin as the condition of enclosure, an inability to understand oneself or to communicate with others. It is the bitter network of fear and its defenses and compensations operative in human experience that lead individuals to actions that hurt themselves and others. In the final analysis, sin in all its forms is a refusal to give back in exchange, an enacted lie about the true nature of reality.

Within the imagery of exchange, the dynamic of this refusal causes the spheres of awareness to close off from

26. Ibid., 170-71. Haughton's approach to grace, especially regarding the universal offer of grace as God's own life, reflects the influence of Rahner's work on her thought.

one another and restricts further response to God's offer because the invitation is perceived as a threat. Gradually a whole network of defenses and lies forms to justify the refusal. Eventually, refusal appears normal or even good because the refusal of love blocks the possibility of receiving wisdom.

Unchecked, this inversion of the energy of exchange results in evil. The tremendous power of evil derives from its origin as the power of love turned back on itself in refusal. While the energy ceases to be love, it remains as powerful as ever. Contrary to love, which respects freedom, evil is coercive and uses any means to gain more and more control. In this inverted mind-set, love and exchange have no meaning.

> The perversion of exchange, like the great break-through of love, changes people all through. It does not always do this in an obvious and predictable way, because the situation is complicated by the fact that human beings are capable of becoming accustomed to, and producing compensations for, quite drastic damage. . . . Sin's effects are so widespread that they are the condition of our lives, and its effects are physical, mental, and spiritual.[27]

In several essays written at the height of the Cold War, Haughton used the nuclear industry as a modern example of the distortion effected by the widespread results of sin. She believes it is a reversal of the creative power symbolized and served by the great cathedrals of another age, because in nuclear plants human skill and industry are devoted to energy controlled by a small group of individuals, frequently for their own power ends and only incidentally for the production of electrical power. Nuclear proliferation, she charges, threatens a scenario reminiscent of the biblical myth

---

27. Ibid., 111.

of the Fall. Unfortunately, to protect scientific and economic interests, any amount of minor and major deception about personal and environmental damage seems acceptable.

In more recent works, Haughton has presented the oppression of women in church and society as the fundamental evidence of the power of sin in the world. The rationalization of the plight of women throughout history typifies for her the destructive power of sin to disguise evil as good and to convince unsuspecting people that the false is true. For Haughton, sin is ultimately a question of the perennial human temptation to seek pseudo-divine power.

In Haughton's theological model, the tension between grace and sin was not destroyed by the resurrection of Jesus. Rather, in Jesus, it was ruptured at the point of greatest tension or awareness. The effects of Jesus' breakthrough continue to be experienced by every human being, and indeed all creation, in the deflection of the power of evil by those who constitute the Church, the body of Christ extending through history.

The gradual process of heightening the tension between grace and sin toward a final and total victory of God's love continues as the process of resurrection is at work in time and space. Each person contributes to or hinders this saving process during his or her lifetime. Meanwhile, until the final victory, the world of material reality remains under the power of sin, the enticement to reject exchange and transformation. Meanwhile, the gospel shows us how to break through the boundaries of sin.

This grace-and-sin tension is a fundamental concept in Haughton's approach to human experience. Her hope-filled perspective makes way for a positive and creative personal expression of faith in response to God's initiative for personal transformation and for the transformation of society and the world. This in turn provides the basis for a practical and contemporary understanding of Christian faith.

Human Development

In Haughton's understanding of creation, grace, and sin, the goal of human life is transformation, or full conversion, which is fostered by freely responding to the offer of exchanged life and choosing to live in a way that leads toward transformation. In the context of a graced humanity struggling to accept rather than reject God's offer of exchange, human development involves an increasing liberation from the human tendency to sin and a deepening capacity for cooperation with God's sustaining presence.

Human development occurs through a series of breakthroughs forged in the situations that life presents. As Haughton notes, this is an unpredictable process:

> Our whole human life is not an even progression but rather a series of cycles of growth, consisting of episodes of breakthrough to new levels or "spheres" of being, with stages between of using and "exploring" the new sphere, until a time comes when further breakthrough is needed if development is to continue.[28]

Haughton envisions an ongoing and cyclic process of human development in which there is no predetermined, magical, or controllable moment or event that guarantees wholeness. Movement toward wholeness is facilitated by formation and is marked by stages of transformation, two related although separate dimensions of the process of human development.

In Haughton's terminology, formation is the familial and cultural influence on the individual that ideally provides the framework for ordinary human maturation. It encompasses law, tradition, education, and convention. By fostering self-understanding, personal talents and insights, and social adjustment, good formation brings a person to the

---

28. Ibid., 65.

threshold of transformation and prepares the individual to handle the transforming power of love in all its dimensions. For example, the shaping of love is ideally the function of marriage as a formative institution in society. The continuous transformative cycle of love is supported by the social structure of marriage.

Transformation, on the other hand, is a passionate leap in the dark that cuts across these horizontal patterns in a breakthrough of inner power. Instead of the gradual development of human potential and virtues fostered by formation, transformation entails a total personal revolution in which the death of a partial self leads to the birth of the whole self, healed, renewed, and restored.[29] Transformation begins with an openness to exchange, often in the form of repentance, and is worked out in conversion, which Haughton defines as a process of self-discovery that comes through conflict and encounter and implies both formation and transformation.[30] Transformation involves a practical change of viewpoint and results in a new way of living, or fully converted life.

Haughton distinguishes four stages in the pattern of transforming breakthrough. First, the remote preparation, a probably lengthy process of normal life experience, generates a sense of desire or longing that inclines the individual toward something at least vaguely corresponding to trans-

---

29. Although Haughton does not mention Thomas Merton's notion of the true and false self, her familiarity with Merton's work seems to be reflected in her concept of the whole self as an integrated, ego-transcended dimension of the person moved by grace to self-surrender.

30. Haughton does not strictly distinguish breakthrough, transformation, and conversion. They are interrelated elements of the process of exchange. As a whole, her concepts bear a similarity to Bernard Lonergan's notion of conversion in *Method in Theology*. Where Lonergan describes intellectual, moral, and religious conversion, Haughton speaks of awareness, choice, and action.

formation. Second, in the immediate preparation this vague longing becomes intense passion when something or someone creates the weak or vulnerable spot at which breakthrough can occur. This catalyst can be simple, a book or movie, a vacation, or a special person, for instance. It can also be chaotic, traumatic, or simply the gradual intensification of the normal formative influences. Third, the actual breakthrough occurs in the often painful self-giving response to the offer of some intensely desired wholeness. Fourth, the frequently overlooked final phase involves the interpretation of the experience of breakthrough and its ultimate integration into the person's developmental process. This integration is usually influenced by the cultural contexts of the person's life. In traumatic circumstances, the transformation process may be telescoped into brief but extraordinary transforming moments.

The condition for continued transformation is a habitual, implicit or explicit, search or desire for greater participation in the exchange of life. Final transformation, or full conversion, represents the total acceptance of exchange. It is transformation in this sense that Haughton perceives as the personal salvation event. Transformation, as the horizon of the gradual conversion process, is not limited to times of spiritual crisis or the heights of prayer. It is more likely to break into consciousness at unexpected points of vulnerability in everyday life.

Haughton emphasizes the essential yet discontinuous relationship between formation and transformation:

> Without the long process of formation there could be
> no transformation, yet no amount of careful formation
> can transform. Transformation is a timeless point of
> decision, yet it can only operate in the personality
> formed through time-conditioned stages of develop-

ment, and its effects can only be worked out in terms of that formation.[31]

Formation can only give way to transformation in time, that is, in stages, as the total context of the person's life allows. This means that although a passionate response is a response of the total person, it is incomplete at any given stage of life. As the stages of transformation succeed each other, the unconverted areas of the person must continue to live and be formed by the law and other external structures.

Furthermore, transformation cannot be forced by human effort since the divine-human relationship is one that God initiates and principally effects. Also, transformation is limited or shaped both by the type of formation to which the person has been exposed, that is, its philosophy and expectations, and by the person's understanding of the offer of salvation. In this context, Haughton emphasizes the role of general and religious education of children in developing openness to transformation.

Haughton also distinguishes between improvement and transformation. Improvement is reform, the preservation, strengthening, and even renewal of given formative structures, putting the new vision into existing frameworks. Transformation, on the other hand, involves a decision to adopt new ways of living appropriate to the changed perception of reality. This demands letting go of familiar patterns and trusting the exchange.

Haughton notes that although legitimate power in a society preserves the social order, this is only the peace that the world can give – order through law. If the law is good, it provides formation, but no law can satisfy the human need for transformation. Although formation is necessary for human society to function, if one remains de-

---

31. Haughton, *Transformation of Man*, 31-32.

pendent on its influence, it leads not to life but to the death of love by asphyxiation. In other words, transformation can become blocked by the very formation intended to facilitate its breakthrough if the formation does not lead to an integrated personal freedom.

In Haughton's opinion, the arena of the search for wholeness is primarily that of human relationships because the interaction of relationships develops our capacity for exchange. Consequently, she consistently stresses the importance of love in the process of human development. This correlation between healthy human relationships and potential for transformation testifies to the, importance of all human interaction, including friendship, sexuality, family life, and broader social relationships. It affirms the significance of daily routines, the sacredness of family life, and the value of human work.

In particular, Haughton consistently emphasizes sexuality as an integral dimension of being human. She believes Christians are called to take their embodiment seriously and to recognize that their sexual reality is holy because it is God's power working in them:

> Sexuality is oneself and is exchange with others in all kinds of ways, as it exchanges with God in them, because the specifically sexual is simply a point of most vivid awareness of the way in which we are our bodies. Therefore, in its less specific but equally vital ways, we know each person sexually, by sight and smell and touch, by concrete service and emotional response.[32]

Men and women are called to be holy, not despite their sexuality, but precisely as embodied persons.

---

32. Haughton, *The Passionate God*, 294.

As an intrinsic symbol, both of the unity of the body and of the passion of the divine-human exchange, human sexuality rightly understood illuminates all of human life. At the same time, it provides a weak spot, a point of vulnerability, at which new life can break through. Haughton notes that as the most intimate and far-reaching human encounter, the sexual encounter is both dangerous and potentially the most life-changing relationship of all.

Haughton believes that for those who are celibate, either by force of circumstances or by choice, if their celibacy is to be life-giving it must be a fully sexed, although not genital, response to the passion of life. Referring to the single states of life, she also indicates:

> Any "substitute" must be capable of providing the same psychological conditions as sexual passion. It must provide both a symbol to focus the impulse of passion, and an activity which is related to the symbol and serves to embody the relationship in concrete, practical terms.[33]

In Haughton's mind, both marriage vows and vows of celibacy are not so much statements of choices made and promises given as they are acknowledgments of how people experience their bodily being.

In Haughton's view of human existence, Christianity is concerned with the conditions for the achievement of human wholeness in freedom. It illuminates the search for fully human and transformed life because Christian revelation gives focus and purpose to the striving by describing the relationship between the human desire for wholeness and the religious sense of salvation.

In summary, Haughton's Christian anthropology views the human person as a whole, composed of body and spirit,

---

33. Haughton, *On Trying to Be Human*, 108.

free although limited, and created by God's passionate desire to exchange life. The dynamic relationship that she perceives between God and human beings provides the foundation for her theology.

Haughton's Theological Concepts

While Haughton's theological work is not academic systematic theology, it is, as the renowned Jesuit theologian Bernard Lonergan indicates, conscious and careful reflection on the transcendent dimension of human experience, the divine-human relationship.[34] Employing the model of exchange and the language of romantic love, Haughton attempts to communicate the explanation of reality that she perceives in Jesus' life and teaching.

The development of Haughton's theological understanding parallels the major periods in her life. Her thought moves from the rather naive faith of a new convert and young wife and mother to the seasoned and critical faith of a survivor of personal struggles and faith questions. Although Haughton's writing has always highlighted women's contributions to Christianity, since 1980 it has incorporated a consciously feminist critical stance toward the Christian tradition and a strong commitment to action on behalf of

---

34. Haughton is convinced that theological discussion is often ineffective due to the loss of a sense of myth and the real human experience it can express. Bernard Lonergan says that Haughton does not do theology in the sense of a functional specialty but as an objectification of religious experience. See Lonergan's conversations with Pierrot Lambert, Charlotte Tansey, and Cathleen Going in *Caring about Meaning: Patterns in the Life of Bernard Lonergan* (Montreal: Thomas More Institute, 1982), 206. He also says, "She calls it fantasy and poetry, but it is an eyeopener for most people, I think. Here is something that makes the story of Christ's life highly intelligible" (151).

justice as expressions of a more radical and inclusive vision of the gospel.

Although Haughton's theological understanding has developed in response to her experience and study, many of her early insights and convictions have endured as foundations of her theological analysis. The following survey of her approach to major Christian themes is drawn primarily from her more recent and deliberately theological writings, particularly *The Passionate God*.

God – Encompassing Web of Love

Haughton's explanation of being in terms of love and of all reality as participation in a dynamic divine exchange of love leads her to understand the nature of God as the transcendent Love that encompasses the entire moving web of all exchanged life. For people of faith, "God" names the mystery people experience as the source of their deepest restless feelings and nostalgias. She notes that while most people dismiss these feelings as a distraction from the duties and necessities of life, others – deliberately or reluctantly – recognize their significance, wonder about them, perhaps name them, and try in some way to discover their source. The naming of this source allows for a purposeful instead of an aimless search, whether the source is called art, or freedom, or God.

While the nature of God cannot be defined, the model of reality as exchange implies for Haughton that the life of God can be envisioned by recognizing that its operation is the same as the operation of exchanged love in our own bodies and minds and in other kinds of life and even in non-living matter. The voice of God within, in the depths of the human person, can be heard by listening to human events and reactions in the right way. The experience of God is especially present in friendship, and most fully so in the committed and sexually expressed love of marriage. Ultimately, Haughton affirms, all creation offers an image of the giving and receiving of life in God.

It is Haughton's conviction that affirming human experience, both personal and especially major collective experience, teaches us that God's love is essentially faithful and passionate but not coercive. The same passionate love that impelled God to become incarnate also hears the cry of the poor and moves people to act on their behalf. At the same time, Haughton warns, God is not a tame God whose actions can be predicted or controlled. It is God, understood particularly as Wisdom, who leads humankind through the wilderness of life's challenges and expresses motherly concern that all people find a home and a livelihood.

Haughton's understanding of God as dynamic Love leads directly to her envisioning the Three-in-One, the Trinity, as an image of the exchange of love in Godself. In her view, the traditional doctrine of the Trinity expresses the nature of God as love, really as an exchange of love, because only if God's love is essentially passionate does Trinity have any meaning. The doctrine of the Trinity is baffling, Haughton admits, and not all the shamrocks in Ireland, or linked circles, or icons get at the heart of the mystery. For her, it means that when we give of ourselves for the life of the world until all has been poured out, the nothing that remains is eternal life, the giving and receiving of perfect love which is the Three-in-One. Haughton suggests that the mystery of the Trinity is opened up from the inside by the mystics who look into the heart of Jesus and know the passion of love at the inmost reality of the Three-in-One.

Jesus – Divine Wisdom and Human Being

Jesus, as the passionate eruption of God's love in history, stands as the axis of all Haughton's theological discussion.

Both her guiding question, "What difference did the resurrection of Jesus make?" and her conviction that the incarnation is to be taken seriously derive their force from her belief in the centrality of Jesus to God's plan of salvation. Jesus is both the glory of God and the one human being who knew how to respond fully to God's offer of exchange and who revealed the reality bonding all things.

Once again using exchange as the model of reality and the language of romance, Haughton describes the incarnation as the definitive example of breakthrough. As the concrete mystery of divine flesh-taking, the incarnation involves every level of reality from the most basic particles to the ultimate Being of God. Haughton describes the impact of the incarnation on creation in this way:

> Jesus was the eruption of God into creation, not just as immanent but as explicit, human fact. This is not a reversible process. It could and did have effects both backward and forward in time, but it could not *retire* from time. To "return to the Father" did not mean that Jesus, having finished his work, simply went home like some tired commuter. A human body, a human person, is *in* creation – enmeshed with it totally – and Jesus was, from the moment of his conception, *in* creation in that sense. By being in it, he altered its composition radically and permanently, and the moment at which the effect of that alteration became operative was the moment of his death.[35]

The history of Israel, God's relationship with the Chosen People, provided the remote preparation for this breakthrough. The immediate preparation for this singular and particular exchange of God's passionate love with humanity came in the convergence of stresses under the Roman occupation which produced the weak spot in time, personi-

---

35. Haughton, *The Passionate God*, 164.

fied in Mary. At the Incarnation, Jesus becomes the place in and through which divine love is poured out in the world.

In Haughton's theological model, Jesus is a unique breakthrough both in his being God enfleshed and in his human life in which he broke through fear and blindness on every level. He is both the full expression of God's passionate love and a real human being living in the world permeated by the condition of sin. Consequently, Jesus' total giving in surrender to death and his complete receiving of God's love in exchanged life overcome the power of sin and break open the exchange of love for all people.

Haughton sees Jesus' entire life marked by the passionate character of the Incarnation. At the same time, as a fully human life, she notes, it was a series of cycles of growth in which various breakthroughs to new levels of transformation took place. To demonstrate this point, she carefully examines a number of scriptural passages, for example, the account of the interaction between Jesus and Mary at Cana. She sees the accounts of the Transfiguration as particularly significant analyses of Jesus' growing realization of who he was and the meaning of his mission.

In exchange terms, the extraordinary experience of the Transfiguration had its remote preparation in the events of Jesus' early public life. Haughton traces the immediate buildup for the Transfiguration from his reading of the messianic text from Isaiah in the synagogue, through the miracles, the feeding of the crowd, and the consequent acclamation of the people, up to Peter's profession of faith, "You are the Christ." When Jesus withdrew to reflect on the significance of these events, he encountered the Living One from whom all power comes. This experience forced a breakthrough to another sphere for Jesus, where the doors between mortality and immortality were blown open.

It is Jesus' death, Haughton suggests, which most clearly demonstrates the pain of the kind of love that is capable of breaking barriers. The sense of urgency, often evident in Jesus' public life and increasingly apparent as his death approaches, indicates not only his consciousness of the mounting hostility of the authorities but also, and more importantly, the urgency that the lover feels in seeking a response of love. The focus in all the references of Jesus to his coming suffering and death is on its necessity. While the necessity of passion, the compulsion of love, is self-evident to Jesus, it remains baffling to others, especially to the Twelve, who refused to believe that the failure and degradation of which he continually warned them could really occur

Haughton points out that Jesus' behavior during his passion indicates something more profound than heroism at work. Jesus is keenly aware of what will probably happen, yet he does not avoid the situation but enters into it with freedom and concern for others:

> There is a detailed attentiveness, an extremity of compassionate awareness of the nature of others' reactions and needs, which we easily overlook because we have heard it all so often. From his concern in Gethsemane for the wounded servant and for the fate of his own followers, to his plea for the men who nailed him to the cross and the assurance of salvation to his fellow sufferer, the impulse of his whole being is a love poured out in detailed, personal care as it was poured out in the gift of his body to destruction. He did not merely surrender to death; he gave himself away, body and mind and human heart, all one gift.[36]

In Haughton's Christology, Jesus' death was redemptive because, although the power of evil had its way in destroying him, his self-gift of love could not be grasped by evil for which love means nothing:

---

36. Ibid., 147-48.

The power of death is sin, and sin is that "defended-ness" of human nature which keeps love confined. Where there is no sin, death finds nothing to "grip." Love is exchange of life, and sin, which blocks that exchange, is the place where death can hold on. In dying, Jesus, as it were, released the grip of death's power *to be an evil*.[37]

Haughton notes that the liturgical acclamation, "dying he destroyed our death," compresses this truth into an exclamation of faith.

In order to express the extent of the influence of Jesus' saving death, Haughton emphasizes the universal exchange that takes place as its consequence. In her words,

We have to remember how the model of exchanged life displays for us the infinitely intricate and intimate coinherence of all reality. Jesus was (like all human beings) inherently related, physically and mentally, to all of creation. And this man, Jesus, is the beloved, the one in whom the Father's purpose (necessity, the "must" of passion) is to "unite all things in heaven and on earth." Therefore when the impulse of love drove him to make himself vulnerable to the worst that evil could do . . . the effect of the ultimate impotence of evil in him spreads outwards also to every being with whom he is enmeshed "in heaven, on earth, and under the earth."[38]

The meaning of this destruction of death, Haughton believes, becomes apparent in what is called the resurrection, the ever-extending outflow of divine energy previously dammed up by sin and death. After his death, Jesus' body somehow broke through the barriers of quantitative materiality to a

---

37. Ibid., 152; italics in the original.
38. Ibid.

qualitative materiality, a change that the disciples experienced and attempted to record in the resurrection accounts.

At the Ascension, the next phase of change, Jesus became invisible to his followers, although he promised to remain with them in a real but indescribable way, by the power of his Spirit. The mighty wind and tongues of fire of Pentecost, which represent for Haughton the final stage of the mystery of Jesus' death and resurrection, show again that something fundamental had happened to reality.

It is at this point that Haughton reaches an answer to her central question on the meaning of the resurrection:

> Resurrection is the restoration of "all things in Christ," so that "all things" may be what they are in the movement of the dance of divine Wisdom. . . . And the Church is his Body, because that is where it is known that this incredible fact is the answer to the question people ask each other, or try not to ask: "What is life all about?" But we know the answer, the nature of reality, the meaning of things, only because we are drawn to experience it, in the particularity of the flesh-taking, at the point where the heart of Jesus marks the centre of all the Exchanges of the passionate God.[39]

These words are Haughton's attempt to articulate what she, like Dante, grasped in her own "Beatrician moment," a moment of expanded perception, a wholly other sphere of experience.

In Haughton's theology, Jesus is the prophetic completion of God's plan rather than a necessary atonement for sin. He breaks through the power of sin and death in the fullness of exchanged love rather than through a propitiatory sacrifice. Once Jesus' death destroyed the inner barriers in creation to the exchange of life, the process of resurrection could continue in time and space through countless singular

---

39. Ibid., 173.

and particular breakthroughs, which are all part of the process of resurrection at work in all creation as the restoration of all things in Christ.

Haughton believes that the timing of the completion of God's purpose depends on the conscious decision of human beings who offer themselves to the process and so become very powerful points of exchange. People must be voluntary sharers in the process of transformation. Otherwise, they not only destroy themselves but also endanger the whole pattern of love's exchanges. The community of believers holds a special importance in the process, because, unlike individuals who are limited in time, it continues through history.

Haughton's interpretation of the reign of God announced in the Gospels is rooted in her understanding of Jesus within the framework of the exchange of divine love at the heart of all reality. In this context, the reign of God exists in those times and places where human beings, after the example of Jesus, attempt to respond to God's offer of redemption, of exchanged life. It is in this sense that the reign of God is within us, a fact which, Haughton observes, means that most of us need cracking open!

By defining the reign of God as a way of living in which the ways of God, of love, prevail, Haughton rejects any sense of an imperialistic Christianity. She understands the "Kingdom of Heaven" to be a shorthand description of the fullness of human life toward which Jesus wanted to guide his followers:

> When Jesus said, "the kingdom of Heaven is among you" or "within you," and when he told stories about that "kingdom," he was evidently referring to something very precise and quite ascertainable, something with "edges." There is a border to be crossed, a reality to be "released" from within, a new sphere of being to be experienced. Whether you enter it, mix it in the

dough, eat it, dig it up, release it, plant it – whatever way you treat it, "it" is not vague nor remote but a here-and-now power experienced in the very nature of things, and it is immediately recognizable.[40]

The reign of God proclaimed by Jesus includes bodily reality and its expression in a life lived in freedom, love, joy, peace and patience. It is found by seeking, that is, by removing the barriers to the exchange of love.

Spirit – Breath of Life and of Love

Haughton discusses the Spirit as the power of love within the process of resurrection and in terms of the Wisdom of God. The Spirit is the innermost reality of the Trinity, the very existence of God. She explains this belief also in terms of exchange:

> The love which incarnate Wisdom so longs to give back to the source of his own life is received totally, as it is totally given and returned to its Source and Origin in one unbroken movement of ecstatic joy and thanksgiving, and that joy, that intensity of exchange of Being, is the one called Spirit. That which the Father breathes, speaks, expends is his own being, and it only *is* in being given. Therefore also it only *is* in being received, and the essence of that exchanged being (Exchange itself) is the one who from the generative embrace between Holiness and Wisdom has being as life, gives life and praises life.[41]

The Spirit, the living expression of the divine *amour voulu*, is equally the Spirit of Jesus, which led him into the desert and through which Jesus remains with his followers. The

---

40. Ibid., 141.
41. Ibid., 172.

Spirit remains active in the world, particularly through the Church, which the Spirit energizes and guides.

Haughton believes the Spirit of God is pushing and striving within humanity toward a real, concrete transformation of created being. In her opinion, failure to take this literally has resulted in the disembodiment of Christianity. She also maintains that the Spirit tends to emerge in history at the right time, at the point of openness prepared by weakness for the passionate breakthrough of God's love.

Haughton associates the traditional role of the Spirit as consoler and counselor with the Wisdom of God at work in creation, incarnate in Jesus, and present in the Church: "Wisdom, the God of Jesus, is a power that unites, that transforms, that inspires, moves, sustains, comforts, nourishes. She moves through all creation and is active not against, but within, human hearts and minds, 'making them friends of God and prophets.'"[42] She also perceives Wisdom as the human experience of the feminine aspect of God, which balances the predominantly masculine scriptural image of God. At the same time, she notes that this is not about masculine or feminine qualities in God, but how people experience God.

Mary – the Harvest Loaf

Haughton observes that there are really two portraits of Mary in scripture: the real woman who later disappeared from view, and the Mother of God, the God-bearer who afterward became clothed in layers of mystery. Although at times Mary of Nazareth was almost absorbed into the "Woman clothed with the Sun," she never entirely lost touch with earthly reality. Haughton focuses on the real woman

---

42. Haughton, *Re-Creation of Eve*, 143.

as a model for women who work for freedom from the oppressive dimensions of a sin-redemption theology.

Through the lens of life as exchange Haughton finds renewed meaning in the traditional honor given to Mary by Christians. As the human being through whom God took on flesh, Mary is intimately bound up in God's passionate exchange of life. As the final stage of preparation for the passionate breakthrough of God's love in Jesus, her "yes" exemplifies *amour voulu* at the deepest level, a willed and conscious co-operation in the work of re-creation. In Mary many threads in the web of exchanged life are interwoven:

> Mary is the "handmaid," the slave of the Lord, she is one of the poor, the *anawim* of Yahweh, and so she is the weak spot where God's Romantic passion for human beings, and through them for all creation, could break through. She is earth, body, "medium of exchange," yet she is all three . . . as conscious and fully willed, as active and sensitive, as a real human life.[43]

The moment of breakthrough for Mary of Nazareth, a moment in which a unique demand was made of her, was also the beginning of the breakthrough of salvation for all creation. Her response in love makes her uniquely a place of exchange, the door between the worlds, the gate of heaven, and a vessel of grace.

In an article in which she weaves ecological and women's concerns through some reflections on the Assumption, Haughton draws a nourishing and contemporary image of Mary from the tradition of the harvest loaf. In earlier days, at harvesttime, a time of both anxiety and hope, some of the first wheat was thrashed and ground immediately. The flour was baked into a harvest loaf, which was blessed and displayed in the Church as a symbol of faith in God's

---

43. Haughton, *The Passionate God*, 140.

providence and the fruit of the farmers' labor. Applying the symbol to Mary, Haughton says:

> Mary, mother, virgin, queen, earthly womanhood raised to the divine – is, indeed, our sign of hope. She is a perfect symbol of the patient, careful, skilled work men and women of our time must devote to the earth to make it bear fruit. She is a perfect symbol of the human ability to bear God's life on that fruitful earth, a perfect symbol of all this ordinary, wearisome, but hopeful toil into the harvest of God.[44]

For Haughton, Mary is truly "a great sign in heaven" for Christians because she is the pledge of that harvest, a living harvest loaf.

Haughton perceives a link between the symbolic femaleness of Wisdom, of Israel, of the Church, and of Mary. The traditional Christian liturgical attribution to Mary of the poetic Hebrew descriptions of Wisdom seems to her to be an intuitive expression of the theological reality of Mary, the one in whom Wisdom found her place, the woman from whom God took human life. The association of Mary with the Woman in the Book of Revelation is the result of a definite sense that, whatever her other symbolic associations, she is an inextricable part of the whole drama of salvation.

Haughton points out that the cult of Mary sprang up in the Church precisely during a period of increasingly speculative theology and growing hostility toward women. In exchange terms, Marian devotion emerged into the awareness of the Church in the gap left by the lost sense of women as mediators of Wisdom. It gave ordinary people a language with which to express the wonder of exchange, the marvels of God's faithful love, and the meaning of life, suffering, and death. Culturally, it also carried feminine

44. Rosemary Haughton, "Mary's Body Is Bread, Too," *Sign* 56, no. 3 (November 1976): 33.

consciousness until it was retrieved by the breakthrough of women's movements in more recent times. Devotion to Mary is in itself, in Haughton's opinion, an example of love finding a way through whatever channels are open. In this section on Haughton's theology, we have seen that her work is Christocentric and that she is concerned with Jesus' example and teaching about salvation and the reign of God. She seeks to express Christian faith in terms designed to direct and motivate people to live their lives as real expressions of commitment and involvement in God's work of redeeming exchange. The nature of the Church and its role in this enterprise is of critical importance to Haughton, as we shall see in the next section.

Haughton's Ecclesiology

Haughton's understanding of the Church flows directly from her theology of experience and her interpretation of the incarnation, death, and resurrection of Jesus as the unique and redeeming exchange of God's passionate love. Her vision of church is a particularly important aspect of her theology because it forms the basis for her approach to Christian spirituality as a way of life.

Haughton's autobiographical comments indicate that her interest, even fascination, with the Church originated in her childhood. As an adult, she has experienced church primarily in the context of intentional Christian communities rather than in traditional parish settings. So, it is not surprising that she usually emphasizes the communal rather than the structural aspect of the Church. In a dynamic interaction, her way of living church has both arisen from her convictions and contributed to her further understanding of church.

Haughton's perspective on the Church is the area of her theology that has undergone the most change over the years. In her youth, the Roman Catholic Church appeared to be an intellectually satisfying system, a true guide and support in life, and an answer to her deepest longings. She was drawn to the Church as a community of worship and as a base for mutual support among its members. Her adult experiences challenged her idealistic image of the institution and led to a period of disillusionment. She still recalls the shock she felt when she first realized how much of theology, doctrinal definitions, and church law had been influenced by politics and power struggles over the centuries. Eventually, through further scripture study and an introduction to systems theory, she rediscovered the sense of truth and vitality in the whole Catholic experience. In particular, she found a renewed vision for local expressions of church within the framework of the institution and even outside it.

The Nature of the Church

Haughton's enduring central image of the Church is the community gathered in Christ. Over the years, her emphasis has shifted from the eucharistic to the service dimension of this community.

In *The Passionate God*, using her characteristic model of exchange, Haughton defines the Church as the body of Christ, the community that came into existence through the passionate breakthrough of Jesus' death:

> This "body" is a *conscious*, known and knowing organism of exchanged life, so that the Church is nothing other than the *amour voulu* of Jesus at work in individual, concrete men and women, evoking in them a response to the love which "made peace by his death on the cross."[45]

The issue of consciousness is critical for Haughton because in her model no unconscious response is adequate in the encounter with sin that is involved in exchange. She stresses that while salvation is not limited to the Church, the followers of Jesus are conscious of the process of transformation in which they are caught up. Ultimately, through the daily lives of its members, the Church is meant to be the tangible expression of God's love in today's world. It is through the redemptive self-giving of individuals that others come to know the true meaning of Christianity.

As a tangible reality, the Church reflects the diversity of all creation. It is not an elite group of officials or specially talented individuals. Haughton uses the image of a net full of fish, an extremely random catch. Such variety serves the Church well, she says, because, whenever the Roman Catholic Church gets itself enmeshed in one aspect of itself, there are always some people who react strongly and try to redress the imbalance.

Haughton describes the Church, the body of Christ, as a eucharistic community. She draws this image from the New Testament, which in turn reflects the experience of the early Christian communities. The Church is called to be the community in which relationships reflect the image of friends sharing food and life. For Haughton, the theological implication here is that the Church, as the transforming power of the risen life in Christ's body, must strive consciously to recreate this same fullness of human relationships in society. To be the body of Christ in the world, Christians must be about the same thing Jesus was, which is empowering others to be who they truly are, the beloved of God, free people who are not the property of any system.

In language influenced by the Second Vatican Council, Haughton stresses that the eucharistic food of the community

---

45. Haughton, *The Passionate God*, 139.

is not a static gift or an object but the living bread, a reality which is known in the giving and receiving. In terms of her model of exchange, Eucharist belongs to the life of the Resurrection and is the real food, the nourishing exchange, the bond of unity of the Church.

Haughton also believes that membership in the body of Christ is not limited to explicit members of the Church. For her, the body of Christ encompasses all people insofar as they are willing to live in exchange. In saying this, Haughton notes that Paul's use of the words "body of Christ" or "body of the Lord" refers to both the Eucharist and to the people who are called and chosen to be the Church, God's new creation by baptism. Paul does not differentiate between the Church and other people of good will because for him there is no alternative between accepting Christ and refusing him. In this understanding of church, Haughton points out, baptism is much more than a membership cere-mony. It is a poetic action in which powerful symbols of life and death focus our personal vision on the possibility of breakthrough to deeper and glorious levels of being human. Far from being a magical ritual by which the un-baptized is rescued from the power of old gods and devils, the symbolic message of baptism indicates a conscious entrance into the depths of life through a ritual that delib-erately creates a situation in which breakthrough can occur. For this reason, she writes, "The language of baptism is a basic vocabulary which enables people to 'say' what it means to become a Christian."[46] She adds that incorporation into Christ means the person is literally, "in his or her ultimate reality, Christ – not by mystical experience or even by evident holiness, but just by accepting to be what he calls each one to be."[47]

---

46. Ibid., 216.
47. Ibid., 174.

Haughton emphasizes the intimate connection between the communal nature of the Church as the body of Christ and the role of the Eucharist in the Church as the living bread that nourishes the community for mission:

> The Eucharist did not occur as a kind of "bonus," to support and encourage those who were to be Christians, and the Church did not happen because Jesus thought it would be a useful thing to have around, . . . Rather, the Eucharist and the Church are one thing, which happened *to* him.[48]

In Haughton's mind, no separation can exist for Christians between Jesus, Church, Eucharist, and mission.

The Mission of the Church

Haughton believes the mission of the Church is to be the prophetic voice of Christ in the world, the voice that names evil and grieves for humanity's blindness and rejection of exchange. The Church is called to promote the reign of God through justice and love. Therefore, it is primarily the duty of the Church to foster the type of human development that leads toward transformation. She admits that in reality, through a rigid interpretation of the great metaphors and symbols of Christianity, the Church has often presented what at best seems a comforting illusion and at worst a formidable obstacle to real human progress.

Haughton believes that the Church, as institution, has too often invested the majority of its energy and resources in formation as an end in itself rather than in proclaiming the possibility of transformation and encouraging breakthrough to resurrected life. By doing this, the Church distorts its own purpose and makes itself the transcendent reality.

---

48. Ibid., 195.

Then, having lost the true vision, it begins to collapse from within.

Haughton emphasizes that the Church's prophetic mission to announce exchange and to foster the reign of God has to be undertaken in the world, not apart from it, and particularly in relation to the cultural characteristics of each time and place. It is only from the position of total immersion in the world's need for salvation that it has the right to speak, and the likelihood of being heard. It is clear to Haughton that the Church must be present in the world as salt that flavors the whole. To further emphasize that it is only by recognizing its place as part of the world that the Church's prophetic voice will be heard, she adds that the Church must be penitent and admit its own sinfulness.[49]

At the same time, Haughton cautions, the Church responds to the culture not by abandoning the Christian tradition, but by rephrasing the tradition in the language of the continually changing cultural context. As part of this task, the Church is also called not only to critique itself but also to discern or judge the culture according to the mind of Christ. Attempting to be totally relevant is sometimes to deny the gospel, which Haughton stresses must always challenge the status quo.

The Renewed Church

At this point in history, Haughton argues, we cannot hide from the reality that an old world is passing away and what is to come is not yet clear: "What is happening now to the Church is not just a temporary muddle before we find re-formed versions of old ways. . . . It is no use pretending that the Church can plod on, heroically unchanged."[50]

---

49. Haughton, *Transformation of Man*, 253-54.
50. Haughton, *The Passionate God*, 241-42.

The Church as a body, like individual Christians, must be plunged anew into the Lord's death. It must risk reaching out in every age to touch the world with the healing presence of Christ. This is in reality a baptismal process in which death of the old and familiar rises in the birth of the new. This transformation, Haughton points out, is most likely to occur at the vulnerable points or tensions in human history, both personal and institutional. Haughton illustrates this point with a passage from Walter Miller's allegorical novel, *A Canticle for Leibowitz*, which relates the grim tale of life generations after a nuclear holocaust. At the moment of what seems an inevitable second nuclear holocaust, irrepressible new life springs forth in the youthful side of a two-headed mutant woman who offers the Eucharist to a dying abbot caught in the rubble of the collapsed church.

Even though honest and fervent prayers are offered for the future of the Church, Haughton admits, the necessary letting go remains difficult. She wonders, "Can we hear the unexpected answer to our prayers for the Church?" In her opinion,

> The answer to the anguished prayer of the Church has been given, steadily and unobtrusively, and it is now becoming increasingly apparent to those who are prepared to recognize it. But this is harder than it seems for a Church conditioned to recognize the Lord's coming only in categories established by its own conscious mind. For what is happening is not the result of reform or "renewal." . . . What is really happening is that the Body of Christ is living its being and action in new ways, to such a degree that many people will not recognize them. They are not totally different, for this is the same Christ, but he is, as we should expect, behaving in different ways to meet the needs of a radically different situation.[51]

Haughton is convinced that most church leaders have not yet recognized the significance of this phenomenon, which is not so much a revitalization of traditional structures as a new way of *being* church.

Haughton stresses that it requires imagination to free our minds to look at the experience of such a long tradition objectively. While we cannot deny two thousand years of struggle and hope, we should gratefully acknowledge the potential for a paradigmatic shift in our awareness of the message of Jesus and the promise this holds for our world. This shift involves compassion and mutually supportive networks rather than competition and dominance. For the Church, it requires the language of a new concept of reality, radically different from classical categories, which will enable Christianity to grow from its roots with amazing vigor.

Haughton suggests that there are already signs of hope for the renewed Church as it faces the issues that are crushing the old form of Church. She finds the principal sign of hope in the emerging small Christian communities, the Latin American *comunidades de base* and their counterparts around the world. These are, she believes, local house churches in the New Testament sense, centers from which ministry radiates. In these small Christian groups, a new vision of church is already alive. In a 1987 lecture that she gave after receiving the Marianist Award at the University of Dayton, she stated:

> The nature of a church, as opposed to just any kind of community, is to be local, but also to be part of the life-giving network which actually makes it possible for people in the local gatherings to *be* church. . . . It is in places where people are drawn together by the common vision, suffering, struggling, failing, enduring,

---

51. Ibid., 241.

and celebrating, that the tradition is formed, tested and reformed.[52]

This type of church, Haughton believes, is a work of Wisdom. While it requires adequate and enlightened organization, it manifests the work of God as Wisdom, acting from within the world and emerging from it, rooted in particular situations, and incarnate in particular networks of loving relationship.

Another hopeful sign for Haughton is the obviously changed and clear influence of a more feminine consciousness in the emerging Church, which indicates a new degree of integration in the body of Christ in all its members. She believes that the feminine dimension of the human psyche seeks greater compassion, the reduction of patriarchal structures, and a more direct and simple approach to truth. Furthermore, a feminist critique is essential to the renewal of the Church because, due to the exclusively masculine power structure of the Church in the past, it is among the sectors of society most resistant to the new consciousness.[53]

Haughton concludes that if the situation of the Church today is recognized, "it becomes obvious that no rummaging in the filing-cabinets of precedent will provide blue prints for the future. If a response is made at all it has to be radical."[54] The future of the Church demands openness to reality and to new visions. It calls for a willing response to painful grace rather than an avoidance in search of cheap grace. Part of the dying to the old which the Church as a

---

52. Rosemary Haughton, "Re-Discovering Church," University of Dayton, 1987, 10.

53. From her earliest works, Haughton has emphasized and retrieved the history of women in the church. Since the 1980s, she has been an advocate for women's rights. Although she addresses women's issues and the role of women in the church, she does not propose a separate women-church.

54. Haughton, *The Passionate God*, 331.

body has to embrace in this period of history involves becoming the Church of the poor. This is the challenge of today's world.

For Haughton, the degree to which the Church can become consciously aware of Wisdom speaking through history and human experience will be the measure to which the Church will acquire both a new vision and a new spiritual energy. In exchange terms, the resulting vulnerability will provide a point of breakthrough which has never before been possible.

It seems fitting to close this section on Haughton's vision for the Church with one of her metaphors for the Church in this era of change.[55] She describes the contemporary Church as God's chaotic kitchen, that is, as the sometimes messy common space of God's family, the place where people are often comfortable letting down their defenses and where they are exposed to each other and so are forced to recognize their imperfections. In the kitchen people share food, conversation, and warmth as well as negativity and indifference. Out of this living struggle new life and hope emerges. Haughton believes that the contemporary Church, as God's kitchen, can also be a center of renewed life and hope for all people.

Conclusion

In conclusion, Haughton's "theology of experience" shapes a theology from below, which she expresses in a combination of everyday, traditional, and poetic language. From the beginning, Haughton's theological focus turns away from a dogmatic, narrow, individualistic, and defensive interpretation of Catholic doctrine, to reflect the broader biblical,

---

55. Ibid., 295-96, 299.

eccesial, ecumenical, and inclusive understanding of the Catholic tradition set forth by the Second Vatican Council. She seeks to balance the tension between law and grace, institution and charism, and to hear the voice of the Spirit in history. Above all, Haughton envisions a way of being church that directs people toward transformation through exchange of life in God's love and participation in God's saving work in human history.

For Haughton, Christianity is primarily a way of life rather than a system of beliefs. The next chapter examines her understanding of the Christian life, in other words, her spirituality as the lived expression of her theology.

Chapter Four

Moving with the Wind of the Spirit:
Haughton's Christian Spirituality

> *If the Spirit speaks to the listening people of God in the events of history, as well as in Scripture, then a renewed search for the springs of Christian spirituality is probably the most urgent task placed by the Spirit before the renewed Church of our time.*
>
> – Rosemary Haughton, *Theology of Experience*[1]

The contemporary study of Christian spirituality, as we have seen, addresses the experiential foundation and conscious expression of spirituality as a personal response, inspired by the teaching and example of Jesus, to the movement of God's Spirit in history. Contemporary scholarship takes into account the influence of the personal, cultural, and theological contexts within which a person's spirituality develops.

Rosemary Haughton's understanding of Christian spirituality and spiritual development and her vision for a renewed spirituality developed over many years. Her personal experiences stimulated her enduring interest in the meaning of life and the role of the Christian tradition in communicating this meaning. The sense of a numinous reality, which she experienced at an early age, generated a hunger in her for "something important." At the same time, the loneliness and relative isolation of her unconventional childhood de-

---

1. Haughton, *Theology of Experience*, 155.

veloped the reflective side of her naturally bright and inquiring mind. Her teenage choice to embrace Roman Catholicism determined the ecclesial foundation for her spiritual search. The influence of several strong and wise women, notably her grandmother Ethel Thompson and her instructor Mother Raphael, impressed her independent character with an appreciation for the role of women in church and society.

The challenges of Christian life as a wife and the mother of a large family during the 1960s and 1970s forced her to balance her idealism with practicality. The Haughtons' efforts at a family-based Christian community both flowed from and expanded her understanding of the essentially communal nature of Christianity. In more recent years, her experience at Wellspring House has informed and strengthened her political, feminist, and ecological critique of theology and spirituality. Through her adult struggles with inner darkness, difficult family issues, and the disintegration of her sense of religious security, she discovered the deeper resources of the spirit and the role of prayer and inner quiet in the process of spiritual growth.

The broader cultural contexts of Haughton's life also shaped her approach to spirituality, particularly her consciousness of the process of history and the importance of cultural language. The uncertainties of wartime England, added to the instability of her family life, led her to value the deeper meanings of human existence. The human issues raised by the Second World War, by the nuclear threat of the Cold War era, and by the ecological crisis, convinced her of the need for an incarnational spirituality. Numerous lecture tours provided Haughton with a broad exposure to developments in the post-conciliar Church, particularly in English-speaking countries. During the 1970s and 1980s, the rising feminist and ecological movements affirmed her long-standing commitment to women's issues and an ecologically responsible lifestyle.

The theological contexts within which Haughton developed shaped her attitude toward faith as a way of life rather than a set of rules. Although she was introduced to Roman Catholicism in its early twentieth-century expression, with its frequently dualistic understanding of human life, the form of instruction she received encouraged her interest in an incarnational theology. Reflecting on her introduction to spirituality, Haughton recalls:

> My education in spirituality was, if mixed, fairly traditional. I believed profoundly that my spiritual life was what mattered, and that it was something separate from my everyday life, though that could be "sanctified" by dedicating it to God. . . . I lived my life almost entirely inside my head and believed that I was virtuous for so doing.[2]

She is grateful, however, that her instructor, that "tiny frail old nun with soft but shrewd brown eyes," dropped her in at the deep end of Catholic spirituality:

> I was lucky. Not only did I encounter some of the masters of Christian spirituality right from the beginning but my very ignorance prevented me from assuming as many Catholics do, that to "cultivate" any but vocal prayer is a presumptuous attempt to gate-crash a party of the spiritual elite. On the contrary, it was impressed on me by one writer after another that to desire a deep and conscious awareness of God, and get it, was *normal* for a Christian.[3]

Later, through her avid reading of the works of Karl Rahner and other theologians during and since the Second Vatican

---

2. Haughton, "Prophetic Spirituality," 4.

3. Haughton, "Avoiding Vanity Fair," 158-59.

Council, she became familiar with new developments in theology and their implications for a practical spirituality.

In recalling her own spiritual development, Haughton also points to the influence of some of the early Catholic lay community movements in England and France. She believes that her early experience of a practical spirituality, which was innovative yet rooted in the Catholic tradition, enabled her later to avoid the massive sense of disillusionment or the defensive anger that many feel when they are confronted with the radical challenge of Christian spirituality.

Haughton credits Thomas Merton with being one of the most important influences on her spirituality. He provided the bridge by which she crossed to a broader understanding of spirituality, one that emphasized living the Christian life as a full citizen of this world. She saw him as a man who "felt the blowing of the wind, and gave it a human voice." His struggles resonated with her own:

> His life, expressed in successive books, was a process of spiritual discovery. As he moved from that very dualistic and elite notion of spirituality that I had learned and tried to live by, and which he had also embraced, I shared a little of that same revolution, those stages of darkness and disillusion, that rediscovery of faith and that hard journey to a new and much more problematic notion of spirituality. I was faced, as every person of faith must be, with the need to find some way to both symbolize and embody the nature of whatever one means by spirituality.[4]

As her biography reveals, Haughton's visit with Merton at the Abbey of Gethsemani, in October, 1967, was a significant event in her spiritual journey because he encouraged her vision of a family-based community as a form of Christian life being called forth by the Spirit.

---

4. Haughton, "Prophetic Spirituality," 5.

With these contexts in mind, the following sections summarize Haughton's thought on some of the perennially significant issues in the study of Christian spirituality today. These points include her understanding of the nature and goal of spirituality, her concept of holiness and conversion, her perception of spiritual growth and its relationship to human development, and her emphasis on the importance of social consciousness in Christian spirituality.

Haughton's Understanding of Spirituality

Haughton uses the word *spiritual* in the Pauline sense of sensitivity to the movement of God's Spirit in this world. Although she offers few formal definitions of spirituality, her understanding of the term can be identified from her descriptions of fully human Christian life. The gradual shift in her focus on spirituality from piety and good works to the close relationship between human wholeness and Christian holiness, and later to a prophetic spirituality, can be traced in her writing. It is also evident that from the beginning she consistently constructed a balanced and incarnational notion of spirituality that avoids dualisms and combines a consciousness of human weakness with an appreciation for the good in humanity.

Spirituality as a Living Christianity

Haughton invariably rejects any concept of spirituality as a specialized and separate kind of living to be cultivated alongside the concerns of simply living. In other words, spirituality means our lives, not something added on to other activities in order to sanctify them and keep ourselves going.

Haughton's early references to spirituality indicate that at that time she closely associated the psychological and spiritual dimensions of the human person. For instance, in 1966 she notes that spiritual development makes us increasingly aware of what is still unauthentic in ourselves and in our relations with others. At the same time, she recognizes and stresses a relationship to God innate in spirituality, which is not implied in or dependent upon psychological processes.

Her recognition of the intimate relationship between the secular and sacred dimensions of life is another significant point in Haughton's understanding of spirituality. For her, the secular aspect of life encompasses all the day-to-day business and routines of life. Any form or expression of a conscious awareness of God in one's life forms part of the sacred dimension. Although she distinguishes between these aspects of life, she insists on their inter-relationship as two facets of human experience. Referring to Jesus' injunction to "give to Caesar what is Caesar's, and to God what is God's," (Mt. 22:21) she explains:

> [This] is not simply a recommendation to keep the sacred and secular each to their own spheres. It is rather a recognition of the fact that the world and the spirit must both be considered, but that to confuse them is of benefit to neither. To reduce the impulse towards freedom to an attempt to establish better and better social and political systems is to confuse the two; but to despise or ignore the structure of public morality and responsibility in favor of esoteric and exclusive soul-cultivation is to cripple the spirit rather than to free it.[5]

---

5. Haughton, *On Trying to Be Human*, 119.

For Haughton, Christian wholeness requires a balance between the ordinary experiences of life and a recognition of the deeper, spiritual meaning of life.

In Haughton's understanding of spirituality, spiritual development occurs when the Christian tradition is understood as an interpretation of how life best leads toward human wholeness. Referring to the doctrine of original sin, for instance, she writes:

> Once it is clear that the great themes of the spiritual life refer to verifiable experiences we can begin to ask exactly how redemption comes about, how the spirit sets about its work of transforming the flesh.
>
> This transformation is what Christian life is about, and it is not a simple matter to see how it can happen, because the condition of life in the flesh is such that, quite clearly, we can have no direct experience of the spirit.[6]

Haughton's concern to identify the most authentic core of the human person without either spiritualizing the Christian life or ignoring its transcendent dimension illustrates her commitment to grounding theology and spirituality in experience.

Haughton's holistic concept of spirituality and emphasis on the transformation rather than the denial of human experience is evident in another mid-1960s article in which she writes:

> The Christian faith is not primarily an ethical slant or a system of belief, though it expresses itself in a very definite type of behavior. It is not even a way of life, in the sense of a certain pattern of behavior and relationship. . . . It is a way of life established within the confines of human life as we know it, but designed to transcend it by transforming it from inside outwards.

---

6. Haughton, "Penance and Asceticism," 79.

It is designed to do this not only within the individual but between individuals. Going outwards from them it is designed to include, potentially, all creation in the fullness of Christ so that, finally, the earth shall be filled with the glory of God.[7]

This passage demonstrates not only Haughton's early interest in personal transformation but also her belief in the interdependence of all creation.

Haughton is convinced that authentic spirituality is a way of life that contributes to the building up of God's reign, which involves an effort to transcend the limitations and weaknesses of the human condition. In a reference to mysticism, she notes: "Christian mysticism is rooted in a tradition that sees the final freedom not as a liberation *from* the material but as a transformation *of* the material, which has in it already the seeds of eternal life."[8]

The incarnational thrust of Haughton's spirituality is clearly evident in statements such as, "Spirituality means the way Christians incarnate the Spirit of Christ. Which means the way they live in Christ; which means the way they live, full stop."[9] In expanding this brief comment, she explains that although holiness is possible in every age, the expression of spirituality is subject to cultural influences and even distortions. As an example, she points to the nineteenth-century approach to spirituality:

> "Spirituality" previously had been draped with exotics until it seemed to have no relationship to ordinary life. . . . The reality was somewhat like Victorian furniture covered with plush, fringe, beads, ferns, pictures, embroidery, etc. Nothing so vulgar as a chair leg or a

---

7. Haughton, "The Kingdom of God," 52.
8. Haughton, *The Catholic Thing*, 122.
9. Haughton, *The Changing Church*, 126. Chapter 11 of this work is devoted entirely to spirituality in the post-conciliar Church.

table top to be seen. And in the "spiritual life" the daily facts of money, food, temper, and sex were equally well hidden.[10]

Authentic spirituality, on the contrary, Haughton stresses, must be alive and in touch with reality:

> Catholic spirituality is . . . not a museum treasure, however impressive and venerable, but a live thing. And like all live things its evolution can take odd turns. It is subject to occasional mutations, some of which die out, being temporary freaks, while others prove useful in the changed circumstances, and survive, and provide a common pattern for generations ahead.[11]

For Haughton, in the present era of change, the realization that spirituality is not a curiosity of religious devotion from another age, but just the way people try to live in harmony with the Spirit, facilitates the transition to a renewed spirituality.

Since the late 1970s, Haughton has stressed the broader ecclesial and cultural implications of an incarnational spirituality, particularly in terms of a consciousness of culturally accepted or systemic sin. Her vision of a prophetic spirituality, which will be discussed later in this chapter, sees spirituality as a way of living the Christian message which addresses today's issues and offers hope to a world groping its way into a new millennium.

Haughton's understanding of Christian spirituality can be summarized as a dynamic personal response, shaped by Christian faith, to the living Spirit at work in this world and expressed at one and the same time in personal and ecclesial contexts. Her approach is holistic, incarnational, and pro-

---

10. Ibid., 126.
11. Ibid., 128.

phetic. For Haughton, the fruit of an authentic spirituality is wholeness, that is, holiness.

The Meaning of Holiness

Holiness, understood as the goal of Christian life or spirituality, is a significant factor that must be examined in discussing any spirituality. The meaning of holiness is important because the interpretation and the model of holiness that are proposed influence the understanding of spiritual growth and the lived expression of a spirituality. Haughton's concept of holiness follows from her conviction about the integral nature of the spiritual dimension of the human person and the incarnational and resurrection-oriented foundation of Christianity.

Holiness understood as human wholeness is a consistent theme in Haughton's writing. She views holiness as a conscious integration and maturation of the capacity for human freedom and relationship. For Christians, this maturation process is guided by the message of Jesus and the inspiration of the Spirit and draws its energy from the Christian community. Haughton's understanding of holiness has evolved in concert with the overall development of her Christian perspective.

Although Haughton's early view of Christian holiness reflects her interest at that time in the psychological aspects of spirituality, it also illustrates her desire to get beyond a purely analytical notion of human wholeness to a specifically Christian interpretation, while at the same time grounding Christian holiness in a psychologically sound understanding of human experience. In *On Trying to Be Human,* she writes: "To become holy is to become human. A fully matured and perfected humanity is capable of the vision of God in the life of the resurrection."[12] She stresses that the individual

---

12. Haughton, *On Trying to Be Human*, 33.

Christian is called to holiness through relationships, by helping others to achieve a deeper, fuller humanity. On a broader level, while Christians participate in the universal human striving for meaning, their participation is special because

> each Christian is called to attempt, however feebly, to do the work that Christ did: to serve without tiring, to give without limit, and to witness by word and act to the hope that makes sense of the apparently ridiculous aspirations of a race of fear-ridden, security-craving, suspicious, ambitious and doggedly alive animals.[13]

As Haughton frequently emphasizes, choice and commitment are essential components of this practical Christian holiness.

Haughton is convinced that the resolution of the very real tension between the sacred and the secular dimensions in life does not lie in treating either one as the whole to the detriment the other. Both extremes are equally deadly. She believes that for most people today holiness has to be understood in terms of a holistic "secular sanctity." By this she means that holiness has to be situated in the context of everyday life. In contrast to medieval homogeneous and predominantly agrarian societies, contemporary society cannot be divided into separate although interrelated groups composed of professional holy people, who attend to a separate spiritual realm, and the rest of society, who engage in the "secular" tasks of worldly business.

In Haughton's view, holiness is neither a superlative degree of personal moral excellence nor an ultra-pious or unworldly existence concentrated on prayer, church attendance, and other stereotypically religious behaviors. Both of these approaches discount the incarnational and salvific

---

13. Ibid., 33-34.

value of contributing to the development of human society.
Besides, such spiritualized approaches to holiness ultimately
warp the meaning of charity:

> If a "holy" person in this sense does give service to
> people in need it is assumed that this is done for some
> "religious" reason unrelated to the real person who
> needs help. To such a "holy" person the secular task
> is not intrinsically worthwhile, though no doubt it has
> to be done.[14]

Such otherworldly charity, in Haughton's estimation, is often
a form of spiritual narcissism rather than a true Christian
spirituality that embraces the whole person.

Haughton suggests that an appropriate reinterpretation
of holiness must be based on a faith-filled approach to life
that recognizes God's "life-creating and sustaining power as
the heart of the matter." God is both creator and the deepest
internal reality of every form and aspect of life. True holiness,
therefore, is no less concerned with performing the "secular
task" as well as possible. It sees everyday life as an expression of something greater than itself, something that gives
it a meaning and purpose not external to, but leading beyond
its immediate existence.[15]

For Haughton, only this type of approach to the nature
of reality allows for a sense of wholeness in the ordinary
work of everyday life. From this perspective, "'secular holiness' is no longer a paradox but a reasonably accurate
description of what is needed."[16] She argues that integration
of the sacred and secular is facilitated by a model of church
that connects Christianity through the local church to the
real needs of the people in a particular place or region.

---

14. Ibid., 23-24.
15. Ibid., 23.
16. Ibid., 27.

A more prophetic stance is evident in Haughton's later descriptions of holiness. In a 1980 essay on human rights, she describes holiness as "the cry of utter love and surrender of the whole being to God, by which the glory is perceived and may then be shared."[17] She immediately includes the necessity of social and political awareness in an incarnational holiness:

> [Holiness] is a sharing of vision but of a vision which is incarnate. It is a sharing by word and act, and "act" includes political and social action, and *also* (not as an afterthought but integrally) personal response to the facts perceived, at the level of daily life and its exchanges, and at the level of faith and prayer also.[18]

The language of exchange here brings to mind Haughton's insistence in *The Passionate God* on the enfleshed nature of salvation and on the exchange of life that takes place in relationships.

In her description of holiness, Haughton draws on the acceptance in Roman Catholic theology of the significance of embodiment for good or evil. Holiness as well as sin is expressed through the body. In Haughton's theological language, holiness is the opposite of sinfulness because, while sin is the use of human freedom to reject the offer of exchange, holiness is the use of freedom to respond to the offer of exchange, to reach out and to do good. Such holiness is exhibited, for instance, in the simple care and affection with which a man tends his incapacitated wife. Holiness is also expressed in the many ways in which people fulfill their commitments, assist others in need, or contribute to society. From this perspective, Christian holiness is not beyond the reach of any person. It is possible for all people

17. Haughton, "Christian Theology of Human Rights," 234. She uses "glory" here in the sense of the eschatological glory of Christ.
18. Ibid.

to grow in holiness, regardless of their situation or position in society.

The roster of the saints, Haughton points out, is filled not only with powerful and extraordinary individuals, but also with insignificant and ordinary people who lived their humanity to an extraordinary degree. In suggesting models of secular sanctity, she chooses servants of God whom she considers to be balanced, whole, active lovers of life, whether they were contemplatives, lawyers, activists, parents, or soldiers. In various essays she singles out Thomas More and Baron von Hügel as two family men of great integrity, and Elizabeth of Hungary, Joan of Arc, and Dorothy Day as women who worked for peace against impossible odds. She also names people from various backgrounds whose lives in some way challenged the settled mindsets of their time, including Eloise and Abelard, Margaret of Scotland, Francis and Clare of Assisi, Bernadette Soubirous, Edith Stein, Maximilian Kolbe and Mother Teresa of Calcutta.

For Haughton, a prophetic approach to spirituality, which embraces both the search for a deepened prayer life and an appropriate response to the issues of our time, actually relieves the tension people often experience about holiness. For, as she notes:

> We need no longer struggle anxiously to sanctify the everyday, as if it were otherwise unholy, or feel guilty for having material concerns. The prophetic insight makes it clear that the everyday, lived in the context of the prophetic task, is essentially holy, and working hard over "material" matters is part of the enterprise.[19]

This approach to holiness, Haughton assures us, is neither an evasion of the spiritual task of the mystics nor an escape

---

19. Haughton, "Prophetic Spirituality," 9-10.

into activism. It simply recognizes the authenticity of action and keeps in mind the nature of prophetic mission.

Haughton's concept of holiness is reminiscent of Ireneus's comment that the glory of God is the human person fully alive. For Haughton, to be holy is to be fully alive, both to the realities of human life and to the potential for its transformation. Her model of holiness is the transformed and whole person who has broken through to the vision of the reign of God announced by Jesus and who is willing to work toward the transformation of society.

The Meaning of Conversion

Haughton addresses conversion in terms of repentance, self-discovery, freedom, breakthrough, and transformation. Through conversion the Christian gradually moves deeper into that transformation, which is resurrected life. Haughton distinguishes Christian conversion from purely psychological development by both its foundation in Christ and its expression in the life of the Christian community.

Genuine conversion, Haughton notes, is neither perfect observance of regulations nor a magical transference in which a new symbol system simply replaces an old one. True conversion occurs when a strong awareness of personal sinfulness as resistance to God's grace allows the breakthrough of the spirit in repentance through self-discovery. "It is when the awareness of sin is a personal awareness of one's own refusal to love that it becomes redemptive. Then the pain is no longer a dead weight to be resented but a means to overcome that very state of sin that causes it."[20] Real repentance, therefore, cannot be separated from love because all conversion involves repentance, a turning away from all that obstructs self-giving love.

---

20. Haughton, "Penance and Asceticism," 87.

In the dynamic relationship between love and repentance, it is love that breaks through human weakness and begins the transformation by which the person becomes capable of sharing more deeply in the divine life. Haughton stresses that no matter what circumstances and people are concerned, the Christian idea of conversion means a conversion to Christ and in Christ.[21] It is precisely through gradual conversion or a conversion experience that people discover that Christianity is true, that "the revelation of God in Christ is what life is all about."[22]

Haughton's early reflections on conversion focus on the psychological dimensions of self-discovery as the adult moves toward a freedom rooted in relationship. In *The Transformation of Man* she describes the process by which conversion comes about through some kind of conflict, in some kind of encounter with another person. Through the transformation, which then overtakes a dimension of the personality, the person is drawn into a deeper level of consciousness and wholeness. Haughton believes that the separation in self-discovery comes about in the movement toward giving.[23]

In Haughton's view, conversion embodies the most dramatic and typical form of self-discovery, not in a pious sense, but as breakthrough in relationship:

> Conversion affects the whole person, but a human being is a person only in the degree of this self-awareness, developed in the saving (or damning) encounter. And the effect of conversion is to convert the language of self-understanding, so that a whole area of ordinary living has a new type of awareness.[24]

---

21. Haughton, *Transformation of Man*, 108.
22. Haughton, *The Passionate God*, 4-5.
23. Haughton, *Transformation of Man*, 114.
24. Ibid., 245.

Furthermore, every step of self-discovery in conversion involves a foretaste of the ultimate complete liberation of the
spirit, which she stresses is "a state nobody attains on the
plane of life as we know it, whose sphere is bounded by
appearance."[25]

In the early 1970s, the insights of Transactional Analysis
(TA) confirmed Haughton's belief in the importance of
ordinary formation for genuine conversion, which is neither
short-lived nor false.[26] In Transactional terms, conversion is
essentially the breaking of the Parent script (external authority) to allow the Adult to develop and assume internal
responsibility.[27] Unless a mature consciousness is in charge
of the personality, even if a genuine conversion experience
occurs, it will not last because it cannot be understood
rightly. In the absence of sufficient formation and maturity,
the power and joy released in the conversion experience
remain undirected and chaotic. This type of conversion fits
the scriptural image of a house built of straw or on sand.
In TA language, without a well-developed Adult in control
of the personality, conversion will be subverted and later
lost by the manipulative and impulsive Child.

In Haughton's correlation of conversion in the religious
sense with human development as it is described in TA, false
conversion occurs when a person uncritically substitutes
another language, in the broad sense of a whole way of
thinking, feeling and acting, for the pre-conversion language
that shaped his or her life. In such false conversion, personal

---

25. Ibid., 114.

26. Haughton drew on the work of Thomas Harris, especially *I'm OK,
You're OK: A Practical Guide to Transactional Analysis* (New York:
Harper and Row, 1969) which popularized Eric Berne's *Games People
Play* (New York: Grove Press, 1964). TA analyzes human interactions
in terms of the inner controlling Parent, the self-directing Adult, and
the manipulating inner Child.

27. Haughton, *Liberated Heart*, 139.

responsibility is abdicated rather than developed. The personality is, to some degree at least, dissolved in the experience. This kind of convert becomes so overwhelmed by the conversion experience that nothing else seems important. In TA terms, in false conversion the weak Adult is undermined and the "not OK" Child takes over and then converts or surrenders to the external influence. The new cultural language may be that of a cult or pop culture, or even a religious system or organization. Haughton adds that such false conversions account for the apprehension frequently directed at charismatic or revivalist gatherings, which encourage emotional religious conversion. She believes that solid formation, while it cannot guarantee true conversion, is an essential foundation for genuine conversion in most cases.

Even true conversion will not last, Haughton indicates, unless there is action to develop and express it. Such integration depends not only on the individual but also on the cultural and religious understandings of conversion within which it is interpreted, because they will determine the way in which the conversion is lived out.

The Meaning of Spiritual Growth

Haughton's concept of spiritual growth builds on her understanding of theology, spirituality, holiness, and conversion. Her perspective on each of these concepts is rooted in her belief in the transformation of the individual in Christ as the goal of life. In her model, spiritual growth is integrally related to human development. Spiritual development is the movement of the whole person toward union with God through breakthrough experiences that lead the person through ever deeper levels of transformation and conversion.

In Haughton's view, the essential condition for responding to God's invitation to spiritual growth is a consistent search, explicit or implicit, for the deepest meaning of life.

Unless a person has at least a minimal willingness to recognize a new idea or experience, no discovery can be made,
no growth can take place. Ultimately, searching in this sense
is a gospel imperative because it embodies the desire for
salvation that Jesus demanded when he asked people to be
honest with themselves, to see and hear with their hearts
as well as their eyes and ears. Although searching is as
important for theology and spirituality as it is for scientific
or philosophical inquiry, the search for human wholeness
is more complex because it involves every aspect of being
human – physical, emotional, intellectual, and spiritual. At
the same time, the search for the deeper spiritual meaning
of life is open to all people, regardless of their circumstances.

Characteristically, Haughton initially addresses the experiential and psychological foundations of spiritual growth.
She stresses that it is primarily in the context of formation
that breakthrough occurs. The process by which human
experience is transformed into a suitable instrument for the
expression of the spirit begins in the ordinary formation of
the person. This education is vital because the spirit can
only work through the personality as it actually is. At the
same time, growth cannot be forced. Formation remains a
matter of preparing the capacity to receive the breakthrough
of the spirit. Haughton is quite clear that no increase in the
practice of virtues acquired by good education leads auto-
matically to the authentic activity of the spirit. Paradoxically,
it often happens that the more satisfactory and well organ-
ized the material dimensions of life become, the less easily
will the authenticity of the spirit break through.

Alongside the down-to-earth nature of Haughton's approach, there is a definite element of mystery and passivity
in her concept of spiritual development. It occurs in God's
time, at the weak spots, most probably in times and places
least expected. Such weak spots are more likely to occur
during the transitional stages or profound experiences of

life, for instance, during adolescence and experiences of passion, loss, diminishment, or death. Haughton emphasizes that the goal of spiritual growth is to advance in genuine love. The real work of the spirit is to transform the human condition, not to bypass it by an awareness of the spirit which, while it may be quite genuine, is only of value if it helps the real growth of love. In her view, "to become spiritual in the Christian sense is not to become *less* material, but rather to become, as Jesus did by his passionate self-giving, *more* material."[28]

In Haughton's holistic approach to spirituality, although every aspect of human life offers potential for spiritual growth, for most people sexuality provides the most common and powerful opportunity for such breakthrough. Sexual love, as a transforming experience, has obvious links with both conversion and even mystical illumination. In order to appreciate sexuality, she notes, it is necessary to reverse the dualism that considers revulsion toward sex a mark of true piety and modesty, even within marriage:

> We have thought of sex as something which had to be sanctified, brought into the Christian life and made into a means of grace. . . . We must stop thinking in this way. We are not asked to sanctify sex or convert it to Christian use. What we have to do is to discover its sanctity, and find out what it tells us about the meaning of Christian living.[29]

Those who devote themselves to a sexual relationship will be called out of themselves in ways which are often difficult and even painful. This disentangling of the deepest self, a transformational process, is familiar to every saint and mystic as the dark night of the soul. It is also known, Haughton

---

28. Haughton, *The Passionate God*, 326.
29. Haughton, *Holiness of Sex*, 120.

adds, to anyone passionately devoted to a profession or political cause.

Haughton believes that for Catholics the Eucharist also plays a significant role in spiritual development because it involves both formation and transformation. The formative dimension of the Eucharist lies in the ritual, a carefully planned confrontation with the sacred and with the history of the community through words, actions, and symbols. At the same time, the total language of the Eucharist mediates the power of transformed consciousness. The converting word of the eucharistic celebration brings together the sacred and the secular, not by fusing them but by confronting the participants with the reality of both.

Paradoxically, as the process of spiritual development continues, the pain involved increases rather than decreases because the person becomes more aware of the reality of the spirit and of the limitations of being human. Haughton believes that it is difficult for most people to take the radical imperfection of humanity as personal fact. As they develop a spiritual sensitivity, after their defenses have been broken down, however, they become more fully aware of their sinfulness, recognizing sin as the lie in the soul rather than a surface mark to be wiped away. Although Haughton does not specifically say so, it seems that, in her notion of breakthrough occurring at personal weak spots and of the increasing pain involved in ongoing spiritual growth, she is touching both on Paul's teaching that God's glory shines through human weakness and on the mystics' testimony to the pain of the deeper levels of holiness.

Since at least the mid-1970s, Haughton's references to spiritual growth are usually in the context of the mission of the Church and the need for an alternate spirituality, one which is socially oriented yet personally directed. This shift of emphasis from an individual to an ecclesial perspective is very evident in her essay "Prophetic Spirituality." Here,

Haughton does not deny the necessity of formation, but she stresses formation for service rather than for insight or personal development.

Spiritual growth in this sense, Haughton believes, occurs primarily in the context of small ecclesial communities where personal transformation is encouraged and oriented toward recapturing the vision of the reign of God for the contemporary situation. Spiritual growth involves a new experience of the meaning of God, an awareness that liberates the divine energy in every situation.

Overall, Haughton presents an approach to spiritual growth which is rooted in both an evolving and dynamic process of human development and in incarnational theology. She acknowledges that growth in an authentic, free, and responsible spirituality is not easy:

> Certainly the task is a difficult one; it is hard in terms
> of the personal transformation involved in freeing
> oneself from guilt and fear, and the insecurity that leads
> us to cushion ourselves from the impact of others'
> suffering and our own mortality, and it is difficult to
> the point of near despair in terms of the social trans-
> formation Jesus envisaged, which would create a hu-
> man community in which God is free to be God.[30]

It is a task, however, that Haughton believes has to be undertaken, not only for the sake of the individual but even more so for the sake of humanity and the earth itself.

---

30. Haughton, "Prophetic Spirituality," 11.

Haughton's Vision for a Contemporary Spirituality

In addition to her comments on spirituality, holiness, conversion, and spiritual growth, Haughton's approach to contemporary Christian spirituality is revealed in her discussions of the relationship of Christianity to contemporary culture. This is particularly true of her more recent articles in which she addresses specific issues of contemporary concern.

Haughton believes that the first step in envisioning a contemporary Christian spirituality is to recognize the immensity of the cultural shift in which we are involved and its implications for Christianity.[31] Writing in 1981, she is very conscious that we live in an era of cultural breakdown unprecedented in scale, speed, or depth.

Neither the Reformation itself, nor the separation of Church and state, nor the floundering of the *ancient régime*, neither the emphasis on urban mission as central, nor the attempt to Christianize scientific disciplines have even approached in depth and extent the theological reassessment demanded by the experiences of Western culture in the past four decades.[32]

Haughton notes that earlier cultural certainties have been profoundly shaken by the numbing horrors of the Second World War, the threat of nuclear destruction during

---

31. Haughton, *Theology of Experience*, 37, explains her use of "culture" as "the whole way of life of a particular class, nation or tribe, and it includes those underground currents of fear and hope and inarticulate passion which cannot be fully and consciously expressed but which erupt into poetry, music and painting and make their influence felt." She sees "religion" as "a language *about* the cultural situation, but it is one which relates it to its destiny." In her view, contemporary society is in the process of religion making, even though we do not call it "religion."

32. Haughton, "The Meaning of Marriage," 148.

the Cold War, worldwide political upheaval, and the final collapse of Enlightenment optimism. Exploding technology, the rise of a new colonialism, and an increasingly visible environmental crisis are also factors that she names as causes for a loss of public confidence and a pervasive fear unparalleled in history. The result, she maintains, is a cultural gap in which the cultural language is incapable of carrying the weight of human experience. The situation is not lost, however, because the dismantling of the old consciousness makes possible the emergence of something new.

In her analysis, Haughton speaks about two common societal responses to cultural change that she sees operative today. In the first type of response, people attempt to reassert the absoluteness of the principles on which the traditional ways were founded. They perceive all deviations from the old ways as evil. While they denounce and reject any innovation, they seek to recreate versions of the old ways in the unavoidable new situation. In the other response, people make an effort to develop new alternatives and question not only the traditional ways but also the religious and social underpinnings of the tradition itself.

Haughton believes that the Church, precisely because it is both included in and emerging from its culture, is also undergoing a breakthrough of immense proportions. Here, too, she says, reactions to the loss of former certainties are varied, although they can be grouped into three general types. In the first type of response, those who try to deny the real issues in the situation make

> an attempt to control the situation by becoming part of the dominant structures, either in practice . . . or by identifying with their discernible and overt aims and policies, thus turning "science," "technology" and "progress" into a quasi-divine pantheon. Once these things become gods, they are beyond criticism; therefore,

those who utter criticisms of them can be dismissed or (better still) hunted down as heretics.[33]

This type of reaction, which Haughton calls a sacralization of the cultural imperative, changes the divine image to fit the foreign gods who bring wealth and power. Frequently, this approach employs terms, which were once filled with religious power to express reality, in an abstract jargon that has long lost contact with everyday experience.

In the second type of reaction, also a form of denial, Haughton finds that people try to escape into a private world by focusing almost exclusively on their careers, family, or personal interests as an inviolate area, or by retreating excessively into individual or communal spiritual experience or forms of meditation. Some people become involved in sects, magic, or mystery cults. One form of this religious escapism exists in closed religious systems where people take refuge from uncertainty. Haughton cites as examples some fundamentalist churches, charismatic communities, and rigidly traditional groups.

The escape inward can also be expressed in an exaggerated emphasis on the pursuit of interior peace and a sense of God's presence. While these are inherently good dispositions, Haughton believes they can be used to conceal a fear of decision and a flight from reality. In such cases:

> Frequent retreats, an assertion of the need to "wait on God," become a way to avoid the frightening challenge to Christians of what moral theologians have come to call "structural" or social sin. So spirituality becomes a kind of buffer to protect the person from the real implications of the Christian calling, whether it be discovered in the gospels or in papal social encyclicals.[34]

---

33. Haughton, "Hope for a Tree," 3.
34. Haughton, "Prophetic Spirituality," 6-7.

The element of denial or avoidance of the broader reality is the critical issue here. In most cases, retreats are a means through which people develop their spirituality.

In Haughton's opinion, reactions to the cultural crisis that rely on either control or denial embody dualisms which carefully separate the religious from the political, the sacred from the secular, and the spiritual from the material, in order to separate belief from culture and to maintain or hide from the situation.[35] Because both control and denial divide human life into separate compartments, neither approach provides a basis for an adequate Christian response to the contemporary crisis.

Haughton identifies a third type of response in which, without seeking to control or deny the situation, people search courageously and faithfully for a way through the forest of doubts and questions that their ancestors in faith did not have to confront. This approach, she believes, is the only one that offers a true hope for humanity. She finds this response emerging in the gaps and marginal places produced by the cultural breakdown, where, outside the power structures, like candles in the darkness, voices for an alternative response have a small but significant influence.

The Search for a Renewed Spirituality

In a number of her works, Haughton names factors that she believes indicate the hunger of many Christians today for a

---

35. Haughton, "Belief and Culture," 163. In this regard, Haughton makes the perceptive comment that there are important and carefully orchestrated exceptions to this separation of the sacred from the secular that operate to maintain control over people's everyday lives. She believes it is not accidental that these exceptions in favor of control operate primarily in the areas of leadership, sexuality, and family systems.

renewed spirituality.[36] First, the proliferation of spiritual books, retreat centers, and religious merchandise reflects a desire, even an urgent need, for guidance by people overwhelmed by new technologies and the loss of former certainties. Second, many Catholics looking for a deeper spiritual experience turn to Eastern spiritualities and either import adaptations of Hindu or Buddhist spirituality into their Catholicism, or emigrate spiritually, leaving the Church behind, often without even realizing the existence of a Western mystical tradition. Third, public concern about the environment and the fragility of our earthly home challenges the anthropocentric theology of the past. Fourth, elements of the popular culture express the passionate, enthusiastic side of a people who, no longer always overshadowed by grinding labor and constant fatigue, seek a deeper meaning in life.

In her cultural analysis, Haughton conveys a sense of this being an urgent time, a unique period, which demands a new response to human reality. The widespread concern during the Cold War era about the "nuclear clock" is evident frequently in her writing. More recently she has focused on the ecological crisis. She warns that in these times of global distress it is less possible to evade the way of life which Jesus exemplified and taught.

While there are cultural indications that a new spirituality is needed and that people hunger for a renewed sense of the spiritual, Haughton believes that the predicament of many faithful and thoughtful Christians today is complicated by the type of spirituality which they inherited:

> The spirituality we inherited, for all the richness and holiness it bred, is essentially for the individual. . . . This spirituality puts the full responsibility for the

---

36. See, for instance, "Prophetic Spirituality," 6-7; "Belief and Culture," 161-64; *On Trying to Be Human*, 95; and *Catholic Thing*, 114-15.

search for God and for holiness on the person, though he or she is expected to need direction, and probably the structure of a life specifically designed to support spiritual search. The goal of human life is perceived as personal salvation and if possible holiness, so that even the traditional and energetic Christian commitment to the service of people in need is interpreted as a means to the holiness of the person who serves.[37]

Haughton believes that the prevalence of this privatized approach to spirituality explains why some good and devout people need ways to protect themselves from the frightening challenge of finding new ways to live Christianity in changed times.

Haughton believes that this predicament cries out for a new spiritual breakthrough. Impossible as the task may seem, given the contemporary cultural categories, she is convinced that the imperative remains. "We have to do the struggling, we have to use the categories we have, and stretch them and rearrange them and do peculiar things with them" if the connection between this predicament and the truth which is rooted in the tradition is to be made.[38] The goal is to come to the place where vision and action intersect. The task requires a willingness to live with ambiguity, to be content in the midst of the struggle. In the end, Haughton observes, this is

an experience of homecoming, to the ancient hearth of humankind where our Lady Wisdom lights her fire, offers water for washing and sets her table for the traveller. That sense of home is perhaps the criterion by which we will know that our searching and arguing and losing and finding and grief and hope are some-

---

37. Haughton, "Prophetic Spirituality," 7.
38. Haughton, "Belief and Culture," 177.

how in touch with reality, that in our culture our struggles to say "I believe" are honest and shared.[39]

The breakthrough which the contemporary situation so desperately needs calls individuals and society to enter willingly into the death-life cycle of the transformational process.

Haughton cautions that the process of envisioning a renewed spirituality must include a focus on social awareness. Knowledge is not enough. An authentic renewed spirituality must respond to God's Spirit heard in the deepest longings of the human heart. For Haughton, this radical listening is the primary task of the Church:

> If the Spirit speaks to the listening people of God in the events of history, as well as in Scripture, then a renewed search for the springs of Christian spirituality is probably the most urgent task placed by the Spirit before the renewed Church of our time.[40]

Haughton believes that these springs are located in the people and that it is time to take the lid off the well.

The Church plays an important role in the effort to listen to the Spirit in history, Haughton explains, because

> the visible Church is the listening people. It is not all the people who listen, but it is an identifiable collection of those people who are supposed to be listening to God and acting on what they hear, and who indeed have pledged themselves to do so – though in some cases rather casually, or with extensive reservations. The people must listen to the breathing of the Spirit, even if the message be only whispered, but at this time it rises even to thunder.[41]

---

39. Ibid.
40. Haughton, *Theology of Experience*, 155.
41. Ibid.

The search for the word of God in the events of history has to start where we are. Only then can we discover where to go as the Spirit pushes us through the power of God's word. Haughton emphasizes that in addition to understanding the contemporary culture and listening for God's word in the culture, a renewed spirituality as a response to God in the events and needs of the time requires a clear understanding of the guiding vision of Christianity. Taking the gospel seriously involves

> a thoughtful and ongoing attempt to understand the vision of a transformed earth and heaven that Jesus was proclaiming, but to understand it as he himself was obliged to actualize it in terms of his own cultural and religious experience. This means we need to be in touch with the basic elements which, to him, were the necessary experiences of the fact of God's reign, the jubilee vision, the breaking in of divine energy to heal and transform land, people, community and culture.[42]

Haughton acknowledges that recapturing the vision of Jesus is not easy, yet she believes that when people allow themselves to read and hear with informed imagination, the message does come through with tremendous force and clarity.

Prophetic Spirituality

From Haughton's perspective, only a prophetic spirituality is adequate for the task of listening to the Spirit in the present situation and discovering alternate responses drawn from the Christian tradition. A prophetic spirituality, she explains,

---

42. Haughton, *Song in a Strange Land*, 71.

indicates a way of living in a given place and time, in
such a way as to be in touch with the indwelling spirit
in humankind and its revelation in Jesus. This spirit
calls to justice, peace and joy for all people; this is a
call to grow in that spirit which binds people together,
and together calls them to live in such a way that the
reign of God may come.[43]

Since prayer and politics are inseparable concerns in a
prophetic spirituality, it is possible to use the word spirituality without dualistic or elitist overtones.

Drawing on the work of Walter Brueggemann,
Haughton describes a prophetic spirituality as one that takes
up the interrelated tasks of the prophetic function: to grieve
over and denounce oppression and to envision and announce new possibilities. Both tasks are grounded in the
memory of how God has acted in the past through events
and people and in the trust that God can do so again.[44]

Haughton explains that the first task of prophetic spirituality involves denouncing what is evil, taking on the work
of grief and anger, and calling others to do the same. In
concrete, everyday terms

[this task] calls us to perceive and analyze what is
wrong, to make it evident and known, by writing and
talking about it, by protests and petitions, by any kind
of personal, communal or political action. It calls us
to rage and grieve and feel compassion. It calls us to
be in solidarity with those who are hurt, giving practical
help but also refusing to cover up what is wrong by
pretending that by giving immediate help we are
undoing the evil.[45]

---

43. Haughton, "Prophetic Spirituality," 10.

44. See Walter Brueggemann, *The Prophetic Imagination* (Philadelphia:
Fortress Press, 1978).

45. Haughton, *Song in a Strange Land*, 100.

Just as Jesus grieved over the suffering he encountered and raged against its causes, so Christians must learn and teach the work of grief that enables people to recognize the evil that impedes the reign of God. This sensitivity is essential, Haughton stresses, if people are to break out of the protective numbness that promotes being "kind, law-abiding, secure and spiritually in a coma."[46]

The second task of a prophetic spirituality calls Christians "to announce a different possibility, to see visions and dream dreams, and to energize toward the realization of those visions."[47] Far from a dreamy-eyed undertaking or vague hope, this involves "seeing the stages from here to there; it means planning, learning, and organizing, and long, patient, and faithful work."[48] It is a creative and imaginative process of empowerment. As Haughton explains:

> [Visioning] calls us to have a vision of a different possibility and to support each other in holding fast to that and making it concrete and realizable. It calls us to believe in the transforming power of love in each person, to which Jesus appealed in order to set them free, and to know that this power can indeed create a different world where God is free to be the Abba of Jesus.[49]

Haughton notes that the second task, which is actually a lot more difficult, cannot be undertaken until the task of rage and grief has been thoroughly explored.

Haughton also indicates that, although the significant issues for a prophetic spirituality will vary in different contexts, in every case, both of the prophetic tasks involve

46. Haughton, "Prophetic Spirituality," 11.

47. Ibid.

48. Ibid., 11-12.

49. Haughton, *Song in a Strange Land*, 100.

making certain realities visible. On the one hand, a prophetic spirituality means naming oppression and bringing evil into the light. On the other hand, it means fighting despair and developing new ways of being and relating. The twin tasks of a prophetic spirituality are, in Haughton's view, spiritual tasks in the fullest sense.

> Prophetic spirituality embraces personal spiritual growth and the transformation of the human situation in the one project to which Jesus called his disciples. It is a spirituality whose holiness is simple and integral, not a specialized task for the expert. It is a spirituality that liberates from guilt and anxiety while calling to courage, hope, and the simplicity of lifestyle that free the disciple for the work of the gospel.[50]

Haughton emphasizes that a prophetic spirituality responds to the concrete experiences of human beings in the same way that Jesus did when he denounced a practice of religion which sidestepped the real issues at hand.

> The proclamation of God's will in Jesus is not a call to change human nature but to free it from all that limits, suppresses and sickens it. It is a call to be aware of the artificiality and perverseness of the barriers that separate people and build mistrust and fear between them, and to walk free of them as brothers and sisters and friends.[51]

Haughton points out that this is not a new vision. It is rooted in the biblical prophetic tradition.

> Isaiah's vision of a transformed community in which people build homes, grow gardens in peace, and none die before their time is the same vision that Jesus proclaimed when he denounced oppression and called

---

50. Haughton, "Prophetic Spirituality," 12.
51. Ibid., 10.

all kinds and conditions of men and women to a common table and a common task.[52]

The prophetic vision is also supported, she observes, by Catholic social teaching during the past hundred years. By living a prophetic spirituality, Haughton indicates, the followers of Jesus act in the spirit of the evangelical communities who caught Jesus' vision.

> Their task and their spirituality are one. They are to call the people to grief and repentance, denouncing what is evil, and they are to call them to hope and to action, because something different is possible – the reign of God can transform human life and society if only human beings will believe and accept it.[53]

Haughton admits the task is a difficult one both personally, because it calls for transformation, and socially, because "the powers of evil have so thoroughly persuaded the human race that survival, let alone happiness, can only be achieved by controlling and suppressing other living beings and making them serve the ends of the dominant few."[54]

Although living a prophetic spirituality is difficult, Haughton believes it is natural to the Christian. This explains why people who enter into it find peace and joy, even in the midst of real fear, suffering, and anxiety. She encourages others with the reminder that throughout history the irrepressible prophetic spirit has broken through over and over in people who recaptured the ancient vision of peace and freedom.

52. Ibid., 10-11.
53. Ibid., 8.
54. Ibid., 11.

Developing a Prophetic Spirituality

Creative activities play a significant role in generating new paradigms. For Haughton, storytelling is an important tool in developing a prophetic spirituality. In retrieving old stories and telling new ones, people become aware of their history and identity, of their oppression and liberation. Quite spontaneously, a type of public mourning for social evils emerges and a cry for change rises. Releasing this kind of energy, the power of Wisdom, requires "skills of historical and psychological analysis, skills in group dynamics and in linguistics. . . . the left-brain skills to sift, claim, and proclaim that which the prophetic power has released."[55]

In addition to storytelling, Haughton also often refers to the role of symbol making in shaping alternative and healing responses to the brokenness in today's world. They can be small, personal symbols, group symbols, or expressions of a whole movement. To illustrate her point, she names several feminine artistic symbols of transformation produced in recent years, including the Peace Ribbon, a stitched image of solidarity that stretched five times around the Pentagon, and the huge quilt commemorating the victims of AIDS. She also refers to Judy Chicago's "The Dinner Party," a highly symbolic three-dimensional exhibit composed of thirty-three large ceramic plates on a triangular table, each place setting depicting a woman who influenced the history of her time. She also points to the film *Babette's*

---

55. Haughton, "Belief and Culture," 171-72. Left-brain/right-brain terminology refers to the scientific finding that the left and right hemispheres of the human brain have different dominant strengths, among them linear logic and spatial relationship respectively. Left-brain traits tend to be associated with what has been considered more masculine behavior and right-brain traits with feminine consciousness, regardless of whether these traits occur in men or women.

Feast as a powerful artistic portrayal of a contemporary statement on vocation, reconciliation, and transformation.[56] For Haughton, the way forward to a prophetic spirituality is to search the riches of wisdom in the Church, both in its traditional forms and in the new life sprouting up in the new ecclesial communities. She takes this stance because

> the paradox is that the same Catholic tradition which seeks to limit and restrain symbolic imagination contains within it the motivation to break out and away, the commitment to truth at all costs, and – underlying all that – the centuries-old tradition of aesthetic, affective, mystical and symbolic expression.[57]

It is particularly in the small Christian communities that solidarity for new alternatives in both church and society is developing in response to the movement of the Spirit. Here, community and relationship replace isolation and alienation. Compassion and solidarity grow from prayer and reflection. Haughton maintains that by striving to *be* Church, these new Christian communities are giving a special character to spirituality at this time.[58]

Haughton's Personal Expression of a Prophetic Spirituality

The direction of Haughton's personal expression of a prophetic spirituality has been greatly influenced by her experience at Wellspring House. The plight of women in society, particularly poor and homeless women, and the destruction of the earth have become the central issues in her prophetic critique and vision.

---

56. Ibid., 174-77.
57. Ibid., 169.
58. Haughton, "Spirituality for the Eighties," 34-36.

Like most feminist Christian theologians, Haughton has become convinced that the patriarchal legacy of the oppression of women stands at the center of the web of oppression in Western culture. In her opinion:

Patriarchal control is the practical expression of left brain dominance. It is the expression of the need to order, to contain, to keep control, and perhaps emerges from a primitive fear of the mysterious power of nature which man must resist and contain if he is to survive. The later history of Western culture is the history of the attempt to establish the left brain awareness as the only truthful one, relegating right brain function to the realm of dreams, fantasy, superstition in religion and women.[59]

Because the patterns of inheritance in the patriarchal system are dependent on legitimate heirs and the control of property, the principal victims of the system are the poor, predominantly women and children, and the land.

Haughton notes that the Church, as an institution within Western history, adopted a patriarchal structure which today resists any challenge to its control. Ironically,

the Church, guardian of mystery, is bound to be the structure most mortally afraid of those who actually feel comfortable with mystery, to the point of seeming to de-mystify it. To a left-brain control-system, mystery must remain in a separate realm to which the left-brain system allows limited access.[60]

In particular, the institutional Church resists any outbreak of feminine consciousness that threatens clericalism.

---

59. Haughton, "Belief and Culture," 166. As Elisabeth Schüssler-Fiorenza notes in *Bread Not Stone*, xi-xv, patriarchy includes sexism, racism, classism, clericalism and other forms of exploitation.

60. Ibid.

Haughton argues that the persistence of poverty in developed countries is not an accident. Millions of people are poor in the United States, not because the system does not work, but because it works very well in producing maximum profit for those in control.[61] Low wages increase profit. Those who earn little cannot compete in the market or afford a home or land. Although society allows for some social assistance, it does not challenge the system that perpetuates the cycle of poverty. Through her experience at Wellspring House, Haughton has discovered that

> [employment] training is all for low-paid jobs, to keep the system going. The women continue to have the lowest-paid jobs with the least security, and they will therefore be regarded as at least potentially bad parents, in need of "services" to keep them at some minimum level of social acceptability, under threat of losing their children.[62]

This situation, Haughton declares, is in effect a condition of slavery.

> These are people who are without rights to basic human needs, dependent instead on legal hand-outs and the efforts of non-profit groups (such as Wellspring), people who have no title to land or property, who can be deprived of their children, people who are expected to be "mobile" as the need for cheap labor moves, people who have no security or assured future, people who can be imprisoned either in a mental hospital or a jail if they "over-react" to any of these experiences. Such people are slaves.[63]

61. Haughton, *Song in a Strange Land*, 39. In "The Economics of the Dispossessed," *Religion and Intellectual Life* 4, no. 1 (Fall 1966): 23-33, Haughton examines the impact of the economic system on several representative poor women.

62. Haughton, *Song in a Strange Land*, 40.

Haughton cites the lack of affordable housing as an example of how the comfort, even the livelihood, of the poor is sacrificed to the needs of the rich. The vast majority of U.S. citizens accept as inevitable a market economy in which the demand is for more homes for people with money. So, the supply is created at the expense of the poor.

Haughton's conviction that the systemic causes of poverty must be addressed leads her beyond a "spirituality of poverty" in which people immerse themselves in the life of the poor and befriend the needy without confronting the underlying social injustice. In Haughton's opinion, social welfare programs of any kind tend "to isolate the poor and treat poverty as a discrete phenomenon unrelated to its context."[64]

Haughton identifies three alienating approaches to poverty, which she believes increase rather than alleviate the problem. In what she refers to as the "medical" model, the poor are deemed sick and in need of treatment. In the "moral" approach, the poor are perceived as sinful and lazy and therefore in need of correction. In actuality, she believes, it is the behavior of society that is sick and immoral. She also points to the "theological" model, which wraps the poor in a halo, perceiving their poverty as a special sign of God's blessing.[65]

Through their reading of the gospel, prayer, and social analysis, Haughton and the other members of the Wellspring community have discerned that their call is to strive for a renewed society based on compassion and justice. Consequently, the philosophy of Wellspring House is rooted in a recognition of the gospel imperative to serve the poor and liberate the oppressed.

---

63. Ibid., 40-41.
64. Ibid., 89.
65. Ibid., 84-87.

In *Song in a Strange Land* and other works, Haughton stresses the integral link between poverty and homelessness. She also points out that although the growing feminization of poverty in recent years has added to the oppression of poor women, "there is a sense in which all women, with a few exceptions, are 'homeless,' even if they live in comfortable homes, because they belong to the sex that does not possess, that is, on the contrary, possessed."[66] Actual physical homelessness simply makes visible the reality of many women's situation.

Haughton especially highlights the relationship between homelessness and violence against women, particularly homeless women. Because women are often denied their full rights as equal members of society, they are vulnerable to violence by men who act out of the cultural assumption that women are property. "The homeless are non-owners, dependent possessions, and women are essentially homeless . . . therefore women are subject to punishment if they do not fulfill their one purpose: to satisfy the demands of a male, and of a male dominated society."[67] This, too, in Haughton's view, is a condition of slavery, one in which women hesitate to question their state of dispossession. Since women are expected to find their identity in a male-centered family and society, they internalize the male view of women. Furthermore, she notes, "The experience of powerlessness, of dependence on another not only for home and food but for identity and role, means that women blame themselves when things go wrong."[68]

Haughton points to the feminist analysis which reveals that the situation of women in society is not simply one of

---

66. Ibid., 23.
67. Ibid., 26.
68. Ibid., 28.

the major evils of our culture, past and present; it is the only one:

> It is the only one in the sense that the attitude of mind which countenances the routine subjection and oppression of women is the same attitude which regards domination and exploitation as the natural mode of human relationship to any other being at all. It is the attitude which could regard as normal and necessary the institution of slavery, and the enslavement of anything which serves the pursuit of power.[69]

In a very real sense, she argues, women's struggle is actually the struggle of the entire human race for its own spirit.

Haughton emphasizes that women's emerging consciousness of their own situation is directly linked to their rising awareness of the plight of the planet. In increasing numbers, women in many parts of the world are denouncing the destruction of the earth as well as its people. Like the woman who anointed Jesus' feet in the house of Simon, however, they are often rebuked. They are asked why they waste their time, energy, and money protesting nuclear power, or protecting whales or rainforests? They are told they should go home and spend their resources to keep the system going and give a little to charity.

Haughton identifies a key issue when she points out that women and men who challenge the deployment of weapons or the destruction of ecosystems introduce compassion into politics. In doing so, they go beyond the politically accepted bemoaning of social problems. The system quickly represses such outbreaks of feminine wisdom. She cites the reaction of the British military to the women's peace camp at Greenham Common as evidence

---

69. Haughton, *The Re-Creation of Eve*, 128.

that challenging the system is not tolerated and can be dangerous.

Haughton stresses that since prosperity in patriarchal terms is linked to ownership, the earth is also regarded as property to be used and abused for profit. The voices of those crying out in the wildernesses of concrete and chemicals need to be heeded, she cautions. The relationship between ecology and food supplies must be recognized because common intensive agribusiness methods of farming deplete both the land and the diversity of animal stocks. They also destroy the livelihood of conventional farmers.

In Haughton's view, the use and abuse of land is an integral part of the gospel of Jesus. He respected the earth as the place capable of being God's special dwelling, therefore a place where justice and prosperity should be shared among all. When the natural interdependence of all things is violated, "things fall apart, dry up and are blown away. The water and air become foul, people and animals and fields become sterile, and Mother Gaia dies with those who caused her death, as they have caused the deaths of other women."[70] It is not enough to make lifestyle changes, Haughton stresses. We must also take some action, however small, against the profit-oriented mind-set that places current gains over the long-term survival of ecosystems.

Haughton recalls how the startling first photographs of earth from space sparked a vast public outcry and mourning over the visible pollution of our fragile planetary home. She describes how the androcentric and patriarchal theology of the past is responsible in large measure for the violation of the planet's ecosystem. Although the task of breaking the

70. Haughton, *Song in a Strange Land*, 101. The Gaia hypothesis, conceptualized by British atmospheric chemist James Lovelock, perceives the whole earth as a living being and considers it as a unified whole.

massive denial of the destruction caused by treating the earth as a commodity is a global one, she believes it falls mainly to women "to teach the skills of anger and grief to all the people so that perhaps all may repent, and come home while there is still a home to come to."[71]

In her later works, Haughton frequently describes the present widespread sense of alienation in society as basically a condition of slavery and exile, of which the oppression of women is the major symptom:

> Slavery means being totally subject to the needs and demands of someone else. Exile means having no claim to the land you live in, even if you were born there. It means being a permanent alien.
>
> The two things generally go together, and the realization of the meaning of these two human experiences is the basis for understanding the situation of women, of our society, of our earth, and perhaps a way to change them.[72]

Liberation and homecoming, Haughton emphasizes, are the scriptural counter-images of slavery and exile. Those who make any effort to dismantle oppression must keep in mind, however, that the denial and control which perpetuate the conditions of slavery and exile are rooted in the patriarchal worldview.

Challenging patriarchy, therefore, means bringing to light the complex structures of prosperity and oppression which support it. In Haughton's opinion, the systemic sinful situation underlying these structures can be viewed theologically as a phantom because "the whole vast, apparently indestructible, cultural system which imposes oppression is as unstable as a dream, precisely because it is built on *unreal*, essentially contradictory, *untrue* philosophical and

---

71. Ibid., 145.
72. Ibid., 37-38.

economic and political doctrines."[73] In terms of Haughton's theology, the sin of unjust, phantom structures of oppression lies in their exclusion of the possibility of exchange on which "the whole economy of divine love is based." The strength to resist oppression and the reasons for doing so, Haughton stresses, must come from the deep springs of Wisdom within humanity and from fidelity to what it means to be human, urged on by the memory of God's absolutely faithful love. It is only in the light of such faith that the unreality of the huge and menacing structures of injustice become apparent.

Haughton observes that the roots of patriarchy run deep in Western society, deep enough to have survived many centuries of political and social upheaval with only minor adjustments. Consequently, the current tide of feminism, made possible by unprecedented cultural change, is viewed as a major threat to the established patriarchal system. Those who refuse to deny the situation are persecuted and suppressed. People who identify the links between abuse of women, destruction of the earth, militarism, and poverty are described as threatening to undermine the fabric of society. And so they are, Haughton affirms.

Haughton is convinced that it is no accident that the new consciousness is linked with the experience of women and that the energy to create alternatives and envision a different future is emerging in the cultural gaps where traditional systems have collapsed. The shift in Western consciousness has liberated a new right-brained, intuitive, feminine grasp of the situation because the left-brain analysis is unable to cope with the new data.

---

73. Ibid., 228. Haughton makes this comment in the context of using Psalm 73 as a basis for a theological reflection on the prosperity of the wicked.

In Haughton's view, the right-brain, feminine consciousness is a revolutionary power that calls for a rethinking
of all aspects of life – education, economics, health, industry,
agriculture – so that life on earth may survive. The qualities
required to shape a new future are feminine qualities of
good nurturing, including "compassion, thoughtful remem-
bering, acute awareness and insight, directed by intelligent
courage."[74] Haughton reminds us that these are qualities we
can recognize in Jesus' relationships with women:

> When we get in touch with what happened to those
> women who followed Jesus, in his earthly lifetime and
> later, we find that the attitude of Jesus to women, and
> their response to that, is at the heart of his promise of
> liberation for the whole creation. Because of the refusal
> of the Christian church to follow him in this, his mission
> has not been carried out, except here and there in
> patches.[75]

Haughton believes the task of shaping a prophetic spirituality
is being picked up predominantly by women, assisted by
men who are sensitive to the situation, especially where the
liberating power of the gospel is most clearly at work.

Empowerment is a critical part of the process of moving
from vision to reality. It enables people not only to take
control of their own lives but also to catch the vision of a
different possibility and to work for its fulfillment. At Wellspring House, they have found that a major obstacle to
empowerment is a personal or communal numbness that is
frequently rooted in a false sense of God's will. A notion
of the will of God as a kind of arbitrary magic to be accepted
in hard times is particularly insidious, in Haughton's view,
because it mimics the genuine heroism of true survivors.

---

74. Haughton, *Re-Creation of Eve*, 146.
75. Ibid., 144.

Equally problematic is the idea that God's will is proven by the outcome of events, especially by good fortune. This attitude renders people powerless before oppression, which they are told to accept as a punishment or trial of faith, or as evidence of the eternal struggle of good and evil. Haughton believes that interpretations of the will of God which limit people's freedom have been encouraged

> to establish and maintain the power of the rich over the poor, of men over women, of white over black. . . . It is used to enjoin passive acceptance of injustice, to deprive people of the power of choice and to create a sense of guilt which deprives them of the will to challenge or change their circumstances.[76]

She believes that, while the patience and coping strategies of the dispossessed are admirable, when market forces become another name for God there is need for caution about what is called the "will of God." The scriptural tradition of Jesus and the prophets announces God's will as true justice and freedom for all people.

With respect to fostering empowerment, Haughton stresses the importance of creating alternatives for women in crisis, even while the process of grieving continues, so that they can develop the skills to take charge of their lives. For this reason, the Wellspring community provides a very different type of social atmosphere, a different way of relating and organizing life, from the systems of control and domination to which the women and their children are accustomed. In a family-style setting, the women are encouraged and helped to rebuild their confidence, to learn to communicate their feelings and needs appropriately, to confront their problems, and to establish patterns of responsibility and caring.

---

76. Haughton, *Song in a Strange Land*, 113.

Experiencing community, Haughton believes, enables people to be true to the deepest roots of their personhood because it provides the opportunity for relationship, which she views as the main vehicle for human growth. Being in touch with others is the key to inner freedom and peace – freedom from false guilt and compulsions, from the fear, suspicion, and insecurity that drive people to manipulate and oppress each other and themselves. Haughton sees this inner truthfulness, which is not discovered in solitude, as the gift to each other of those who are aware of God's action in their lives. It is the freedom of which Paul speaks, which springs from love.

Celebrations, holiday observances, storytelling, and ritual provide important opportunities at Wellspring for creating symbols which counteract despair. Singing together affords an important way to release energy and speak of commitment and hope. For Haughton, these activities are part of the prophetic task of putting people in touch with God and announcing new possibilities. As she notes, the same Spirit is at work in the prophets in the desert and in the small ways in which human beings daily bring salvation to each other.

In Haughton's opinion, ritual plays an important role in establishing the visibility of the Church, even on the household level. At Wellspring, which is intentionally ecumenical and inclusive in its prayer, weekly liturgies and the festive observances for Christmas and Holy Week strengthen the community's sense of identity and purpose and provide a common language for expressing hopes and fears. The power of Word and symbol gently opens the possibility for healing and transformation.

Because Haughton perceives liberation not only as a going out but also as a returning home, caring for the earth is a significant part of her use of homecoming as a transforming image. "The earth is home: we have no other," she asserts. "The earth's women are coming to realize that their own age-old dispossession is likely to become the homelessness of all creation, if the earth becomes uninhabitable."[77] For this reason, growing vegetables, preparing nourishing food, recycling, and boycotting certain products are some of the practical signs of Wellspring's commitment to the earth.

In Haughton's mind, there is a definite relationship between alternative theologies, which lead to alternative lifestyles, and alternative spiritualities, which support and interpret both these theologies and lifestyles. As part of her effort to express Christianity in today's terms, Haughton has written extensively on feminist reinterpretations of traditional spiritualities which, although intended for everyone, were developed with the assumption that what was good for men must also be good for women! In reality, some traditional spiritual teachings, such as the portrayal of patience as the passive acceptance of gross injustice, were quite destructive for women.

In reinterpreting other virtues, Haughton suggests that the repentance asked of women today is the renunciation of self-destructive behavior, the non-toleration of abuse, and the refusal to sacrifice career goals or to set aside talents simply to placate someone else.[78] She recommends that women honestly and humbly reclaim the power of self-determination, which is their right.

Haughton finds that endurance, in the sense of perseverance, is a particularly appropriate virtue for prophetic spirituality. She describes endurance as a virtue linked to common sense, honesty, and fidelity, which trusts that there is something worthwhile to be gained by not giving in.

---

77. Ibid., 144.

78. Rosemary Haughton, "Women Should Ponder Before Rending Their Garments," *National Catholic Reporter* 27 (22 February 1991): 2.

Endurance makes a choice and sticks to it for as long as it takes. Endurance enables people to get beyond anger, which sooner or later burns out, and to preserve the warmth of compassion and hope in hard and discouraging circumstances. At the same time, it is not passive endurance, which eventually is self-destructive.

Commitment, which Haughton views as a response to the impulse of the indwelling Spirit toward the fullness of life, is another virtue at the root of a contemporary prophetic spirituality. While public commitment is a symbol of the desired reality, the essence of commitment is the inner response. Commitment is an adventure that takes the person through many stages of growth and honest reassessment. At times, the expression of commitment must change or find a new direction if the original response to the Spirit is to remain alive. As an example of how cultural change may affect the understanding of a commitment, Haughton notes that commitment to human progress, once expressed in scientific enthusiasm, must now involve a collective revolution toward sustainable lifestyles. Patriotism, once a genuine commitment to freedom, is now often a false commitment preserving a destructive way of life and must be redirected. Even Christian commitment, in Haughton's view, must at times seek new forms of expression:

> As Christians, our response to this system of competitive greed must be a profound revolution in spirituality. . . . We have to recommit ourselves in faith and trust to the personal and social tasks which make for health and wholeness for ourselves, our nation, our world.[79]

In Haughton's view, a prophetic spirituality also requires a reexamination of the virtue of poverty. Lack of the

79. Ibid.

basic necessities of life, destitution, is not a virtue and cannot honestly be accepted in any sense as a blessing from God. The poverty that acts as a soil in which Wisdom can grow involves laying aside bias, being vulnerable to the break-through of divine love, accepting the limitations of the human condition, and being hungry for the meaning of life and for God.[80]

Clearly, Haughton is convinced that a prophetic spirituality responds to the need for an adequate contemporary spirituality:

> Prophetic spirituality embraces the search for a deep-ened prayer life, which so many are seeking, together with a sense of the Christian situation that takes for granted a response to the issues of the day in whatever way is possible and appropriate to the person, but it does not leave the individual to wrestle with vocation in a kind of vacuum.[81]

By situating her approach to contemporary spirituality within the prophetic mission of the Church, Haughton grounds her prophetic spirituality in the Christian tradition. In her opin-ion, prophetic spirituality encourages each individual to respond personally to the universal call of the Spirit. At the same time, every individual response becomes part of the whole Christian attempt to conform to the way of the Spirit and to build the reign of God.

It is the Spirit, Haughton believes, who is calling forth a prophetic spirituality at this time. The Spirit summons the Church to be a prophetic community which models the gospel of love and hope in a world full of indifference and even hatred. God's Spirit calls Christians to a holiness that is "intimate, adventurous, deeply and practically compas-

---

80. Haughton, *The Passionate God*, 326-33.
81. Haughton, "Prophetic Spirituality," 9.

sionate, waiting on the Lord in a sensitive and confident obedience."[82] Although the Church does not achieve this goal fully, because it is caught up in the very fears and power struggles which lead to oppression, Haughton believes that

> the heart of the church, the place where it is most fully itself, always had and still has that prophetic character. Now more than ever the prophetic voice and activity are needed, and the prophetic spirituality that makes it possible is simply the way we try to live as followers of Christ. Insofar as we do so we are freed, hallowed and made perfect, together. We don't know when, or how, the fullness of God's reign may be established; we do know that here and now it is being lived, it is visible, unambiguous, and full of energy. It is the fruit of prophetic spirituality.[83]

Prophetic spirituality, in turn, springs forth anew in hope, in accepting the challenge of Jesus, and in following the voice of the Spirit.

Conclusion

Haughton's spirituality emerges from her own faith and hope. It is the result of weaving her insights and experiences into a vision of the possibility of a new breakthrough of God's Spirit in the world during this period of cultural crisis at the end of the twentieth century.

Haughton's spirituality has been incarnational and holistic from the start. As her attention moved first from the psychological to the transcendent and later to the social dimensions of Christian faith, she developed a more pro-

---

82. Haughton, "Spirituality for the Eighties," 44.

83. Haughton, "Prophetic Spirituality," 12.

phetic approach to spirituality. For almost two decades now, she has examined spirituality through the lens of a feminist Christian critique. As a consequence, since 1981 she has devoted her energy primarily to the assistance of homeless women and their children. The Wellspring community and its projects are living expressions of the prophetic spirituality which she advocates.

Haughton's spirituality is also both contemplative and political. Two movements are consistently present and interwoven throughout her exploration of contemporary spirituality. In one movement, she looks inward into the depths of her own experience of human relationships, of Christian faith, and of the Church. In the other movement, she examines human experience and its cultural setting, and the lived expression of Christian faith in everyday life.

Without losing sight of the highest aspirations of Christian faith in the Resurrection, Haughton busies herself with the ordinary tasks that bring the peace and freedom of God's reign into reality. Her spirituality is in touch with the deepest movements of the human heart, the dynamics of human society and the Church, and the wisdom of both scripture and the Christian tradition.

Throughout her life, Haughton's pursuit of the mysterious "something important" has remained grounded in her conviction of the truth of the living Christ, the basis of her hope:

> Neither the past nor the present has a monopoly on sanctity, but whenever human life in its twilight groping is touched by the Spirit who comes to meet us, then it is irradiated by the light of the future in Christ. This is spirituality, and it can take innumerable forms, but under all forms it is recognizable as the presence of Christ.[84]

---

84. Haughton, *Changing Church*, 133-34.

Haughton's spirituality is a committed and intentional way of living everyday life in response to the voice of the Spirit in the world. Through her writings and example she invites others to work toward Jesus' vision of the reign of God as it is announced in the Gospels and reflected in the early Christian communities.

Conclusion

Haughton as a Witness to Hope

The hope, and there is hope, lies in the fact that there have always been two traditions in the history of Christianity. One is the tradition created precisely in order to enable one class of Christians to maintain power and control with a good conscience, . . . The other tradition is the one Jesus began, which we call the prophetic tradition, . , of a people with whom God is at home because there is no oppression or destruction, and the fertility of the land and the productivity of the people express the abundance of God's love shown in creation. . . . [It] provides hope for the future of women in the church and indeed hope for the world.
– Rosemary Haughton, "Women and the Church."[1]

Essentially, a witness is a person who provides evidence of a truth. Since the time of the early church, Christian witnesses have not only given testimony to their belief in Jesus by their words but also with their lives. To describe Rosemary Haughton as a witness to hope is to claim that by her words and actions she demonstrates her belief that the radical message of Jesus remains a source of life and hope for the world. Her role as witness is supported by the fact that her spirituality responds to the realities of the contemporary cultural context, remains true to the Christian tradition, and embodies a prophetic understanding of Christian spirituality.

---

1. Rosemary Haughton, "Women and the Church," *Thought* 66 (December 1991): 403.

179

An informed contemporary cultural consciousness is evident throughout Haughton's work in both her demonstrated knowledge of history and her understanding of the dynamics of culture. She recognizes the immensity of the cultural paradigm shift that is taking place and addresses its impact on the lives of people today. Her critical analysis of social issues, particularly the systemic dimensions of oppression as they relate to the poor, women, and the earth, confronts her readers with the underlying issues and vested interests affecting the fabric of society in general and of the church in particular.

Haughton emphasizes the importance of choice and action, as opposed to denial and passivity, in Christians' response to cultural issues. Through her own counter-cultural choices she has developed a lifestyle which resists the destructive tendencies of modern culture. While twentieth-century culture has promoted individualism, separation, and dominance, she has fostered community, inter-dependence, and partnership. In particular, she has encouraged and modeled holistic approaches to feminist and ecological concerns.

Haughton writes primarily for middle-class Christians in the English-speaking cultures around the North Atlantic. While this restricted focus might appear to be a weakness, it is actually a strength of her work. As Sharon Welch points out, the potential for change is rooted in the particular.[2] Haughton's spirituality is grounded in the common, recognizable experiences of her audience. She expresses her insights into the contemporary situation in terms accessible to the general reader. In this way, her prophetic spirituality offers an alternative perspective to people overwhelmed by

---

2. See Sharon Welch, *Communities of Resistance and Solidarity: A Feminist Theology of Liberation* (Maryknoll: Orbis, 1985), especially her discussion in chap. 5 of the primacy of the particular.

the rapid changes and social crises taking place. The immense popularity of her work, evidenced by the volume of her published material and her many lecture engagements, testifies to her ability to interpret the contemporary context in a meaningful way.

Haughton's spirituality is also an authentic expression of the Christian tradition. Although Haughton did not study theology in a formal way, she reflects the teaching of recognized contemporary theologians such as Karl Rahner, Bernard Lonergan, and Elisabeth Schüssler-Fiorenza. Both her Christocentric and ecclesial approach and her emphasis on human experience and conversion exemplify the theological perspective of Vatican II. Haughton's spirituality also demonstrates many elements of contemporary critical theologies, including liberationist approaches, feminist critique, and ecological sensitivity, which are discussed by well-known authors such as Gustavo Gutiérrez, Rosemary Radford Ruether, and Sallie McFague.

Haughton's most helpful theological insights are found in her creative understanding of grace, the resurrection, and the church. Her interpretations are rooted in her vision of the dynamics of exchange at work throughout creation. Her intuitive grasp of the notion of sin as the refusal of God's offer of grace or exchange of life provides the basis for her positive attitude to cooperation with God's transforming love. Through her stress on the cosmic significance of the incarnation and resurrection of Jesus as evidence of God's redeeming will, she affirms the importance of everyday life as the place of transformation. Her notion of the formative dimension of the church as the primary vehicle for the accomplishment of God's saving purpose gives renewed meaning to membership in the Christian community.

At the same time, Haughton does not hesitate to lay bare the sins of the church, particularly with respect to the limitation of human freedom and the oppression of groups or individuals. She rebukes the church for losing sight of Jesus' vision of an egalitarian and prophetic community. She calls Christians to exercise personal responsibility in their faith and to work for the renewal of the church.

Some critics fault Haughton's use of scripture, find her model of exchange and paradigm of the medieval romance tradition problematic, or express concern that her stress on local churches would lead to an eventual loss of unity within the institutional Church.[3] While it is important to acknowledge the limits of Haughton's theology, it is even more important to recognize the wisdom and balance of her approach, which is grounded in experience and Christian tradition.

Haughton's spirituality also represents a sound and creative expression of contemporary spirituality. Her perception of Christian spirituality as the holistic and free response of the naturally graced person to God's invitation in Jesus through the power of the indwelling Spirit corresponds to the descriptions of contemporary spirituality presented by scholars in the field. Her incorporation of material from psychology, history, science, and sociology, demonstrates a multi-disciplinary approach to spirituality.

Haughton's spirituality presents a balanced, integrated approach to Christian life, which avoids a narrow definition of prayer and a restricted sense of religious experience. She

---

3. Since *The Passionate God* was Haughton's major theological work, it received more critical reviews than her other books. The "Review Symposium" in *Horizons* (Spring 1983) provides a cross-section of reviews of the book. While Pheme Perkins objects to her omission of exegetical concerns and discounts her work as "intellectually inadequate for the task it sets out" (132), Lawrence Cunningham and other reviewers endorse her insight into biblical passages and the crisis of language (130). In his review in *The Irish Theological Quarterly* 49 (1982): 216-17, Noel O'Donoghue notes that the maturity of *The Passionate God* is evidenced in its dealing with death. He also expresses his concern that there be sufficient structure to support the life of the church.

attends to feminist issues and the links between faith, justice, and ecology. She argues for a spirituality that is empowering, compassionate, and inclusive.

Haughton's prophetic spirituality announces the possibility of reversing the trajectory of modern culture toward self-destruction. Her metaphor of homecoming identifies a spirituality concerned with creating space for people caught in the margins and cracks of the cultural situation. Hospitality, a traditional trait of monastic spirituality, is evident in her welcoming of people who are alienated by society. Her focus on fidelity in heart and spirit rather than on loyalty to an institution places discipleship over dogma in the discernment of the movement of God's Spirit today. Her insight goes to the heart of the "catholic enterprise," as she calls it, the transformation of the world.

The Significance of Haughton's Contribution

Haughton addresses the practical implications of Christian teaching, which need to be considered if Christianity is to remain a credible and fruitful instrument of the Spirit. Through her creative analysis of the dynamic love that sustains the universe and which is expressed in the liberating love of Jesus, she presents Christianity as an important resource for human and cultural development. Her appreciation for the role of ritual, symbol, and other religious expressions in community life and inner healing offers a remedy for the general diminishment of symbolic consciousness in the culture.[4]

---

4. Rollo May observes that in periods of rapid change, people lose the sense of personal appropriation of symbol. Reappropriation must be rooted in an understanding of the new culture. See Rollo May, ed., "The Significance of Symbols," in *Symbolism in Religion and Literature* (New York: Braziller, 1960)

Despite her awareness of human weaknesses within the Roman Catholic Church as an institution, Haughton has chosen to remain Catholic and has shown an unfailing, although not uncritical, loyalty to the church. In this respect, she speaks to many Roman Catholics and other Christians, especially women, whose faith in their religious traditions has been challenged by radical changes in almost every aspect of their lives, social, political, and economic as well as religious.

Haughton's contribution to a contemporary pastoral understanding of theology and spirituality is valuable in several areas. First, she makes the perspective of the Second Vatican Council available to the general reader. At the same time, the professional theologian benefits from her fresh insights, the fruit of her long experience of as a lay member of the Church. Second, by describing, questioning, and challenging aspects of theological concepts she encourages Christians, Roman Catholics in particular, to become mature and critical members of the faith community.

Third, Haughton's ecumenical, feminist, and ecological sensitivity, particularly her positive attitude to embodiment and sexuality, contributes to the inclusion of these important elements in pastoral practice. Fourth, she adds to the chorus of women's voices in the church speaking out against oppression in the church as well as in society. Finally, by challenging her audience to rouse themselves out of passivity and become engaged in the process of *being* church, she contributes significantly to the empowerment of the laity envisioned by Vatican II.

Perhaps Haughton's most significant contribution to pastoral theology is her illumination in word and action of the process of everyday transformation. She emphasizes the significance of the seemingly insignificant routines of life and their relationship to the salvific core of Christian teaching. She exemplifies a positive, creative, and practical response to the "signs of the times" as opportunities for growth rather than as portents of doom.

In her spirituality, Haughton goes to the heart of the Christian life by calling for true discipleship and commitment to the ecclesial and human project of promoting sustainable life on earth. She consistently stresses the importance of personal choice and conversion. A major point is her recognition that something has to give if humanity is to break through the present situation, the cultural impasse to which FitzGerald refers. In her opinion, this breakthrough is most likely to come at the cultural weak spot, which today is the place of the poor and the marginalized.

Haughton's life exemplifies the postmodern Christian who, no longer sustained by institutions, is groping for truth and meaning. Faced with the crumbling of the social and religious traditions which she took for granted in her youth, she has reworked and reintegrated her understanding of Christianity. She has converted limits and disappointments into possibilities. Her determination to find new life beyond failed hopes has demanded letting go of some of her dreams, mourning losses she had not anticipated, and going where she had never expected to go. In her openness to God, Haughton affirms the possibility of life guided by the Spirit.

In her approach, Haughton penetrates the shell of routine in experience and the density of theological concepts to reveal the dynamics of the universe in operation. She invites others to undertake their own transforming journeys. In her restless pursuit for meaning, she has often gone against the tide of culture. Her search has brought her face-to-face with the impasse in which contemporary society is caught. As a result of her choice not to deny or avoid the situation, she has been responsibly involved in alternative approaches to today's problems. In many areas, such as her concern for the earth, she has been ahead of her time.

In company with the wise people of every generation, Haughton continues in the human journey toward the reign of God. In the very applicable ancient metaphor, her vision encompasses a return of all people from exile to God's homeland of peace and justice.

Selected Bibliography

Primary Sources

The following pages provide a comprehensive bibliography of Rosemary Haughton's published material for adults on religious and theological topics, in chronological order.

Books

Six Saints for Parents. London: Burns & Oates, 1962; New York: Sheed & Ward, 1963.

Christian Responsibility. New York: Sheed & Ward, 1964.

Beginning Life in Christ: The Gospel in Christian Education. New York: Newman Press, 1966.

Married Love in Christian Life. London: Burns & Oates, 1966.

On Trying to Be Human. Springfield, Ill.: Templegate, 1966.

The Transformation of Man: A Study of Conversion and Community. London: Chapman, 1967; revised edition, Springfield, Ill.: Templegate, 1980.

Dialogue: The State of the Church Today. New York: Sheed & Ward, 1967; London: Chapman, 1968. With Cardinal Heenan.

Elizabeth's Greeting. Philadelphia: Lippincott, 1968.

Problems of Christian Marriage. New York: Paulist, 1968.

Why Be a Christian? London: G. Chapman, 1968; Lippincott, 1968.

Act of Love. London: Chapman, 1968; Philadelphia: Lippincott, 1969.

The Changing Church. London: Chapman, 1969.

The Holiness of Sex. St. Meinrad, Ind.: Abbey, 1969.

The Gospel Where It Hits Us: Christianity and Contemporary Concerns. London: Chapman, 1969.

Love. London: C. A. Watts & Company, 1970.

Where Do We Go from Here? A Family Stocktaking on Christian Education. London: Chapman, 1970.

Theology of Marriage. Theology Today Series, no. 31. Notre Dame, Ind.: Fides, 1971.

In Search of Tomorrow: A Future to Live In. St. Meinrad, Ind.: Abbey, 1972.

The Mystery of Sexuality. New York: Paulist, 1972.

The Knife-Edge of Experience. London: Darton, Longman & Todd, 1972. Published as *The Theology of Experience.* New York: Paulist, 1972, 1975.

Tales from Eternity: The World of Faerie and the Spiritual Search. Allen & Unwin, 1973; New York: Seabury, 1974.

The Liberated Heart: Transactional Analysis in Religious Experience. London: Chapman, 1975; New York: Seabury, 1974.

The Drama of Salvation. New York: Seabury, 1975; London: S.P.C.K., 1976.

Feminine Spirituality. New York: Paulist, 1976.

The Catholic Thing. Springfield, Ill.: Templegate, 1980.

The Passionate God. Mahwah, N.J.: Paulist, 1981; London: Darton, Longman and Todd, 1981.

The Re-Creation of Eve. Springfield, Ill.: Templegate, 1985.

Song in a Strange Land. Springfield, Ill.: Templegate, 1990.

The Tower that Fell. Mahwah, N.J.: Paulist, forthcoming 1997.

Images for Change: A Vision of a Hospitable Future. Mahwah: N.J.: Paulist, forthcoming 1997.

Pamphlets and Study Paper

Christian Sex Education. London: Ealing Abbey, 1966.
What Is a Family? London: Ealing Abbey, 1966.
What Is Marriage? London: Ealing Abbey, n.d.
Who Is My Neighbor? London: Ealing Abbey, 1966.
Being a Christian Family. London: Ealing Abbey, 1967.
Being a Christian Now. London: Ealing Abbey, 1967.
Rebellious Christians. London: Ealing Abbey, 1967.
New Look Celibacy. Synthesis Series, no. 19. Chicago: Fran-
ciscan Herald Press, 1970.
Re-Discovering Church. Dayton: University of Dayton Press,
1987.
The Church as Prophet: Challenge, and Judgement, Warren
Lecture Series. Tulsa: University of Tulsa Press, 1989.
"'There Is Hope for a Tree': A Study Paper on the Emerging
Church." In The Living Edge of Christianity series.
Vol. 1, no. 3, 1-60. Washington, D.C.: Christianity in
a New Key, 1981.

Chapters in Edited Works

"Penance and Asceticism in the Modern World." In *Sin and
Repentance*, ed. Denis O'Callaghan, 73-92. Dublin: M.
H. Gill and Son, 1967.
"Avoiding Vanity Fair." In *On the Run*, ed. Michael F.
McCauley, 156-57. Chicago: Thomas More, 1974.
"Theology of Marriage." In *Male and Female: Christian
Approaches to Sexuality*, ed. Ruth Tiffany Barnhouse
and Urban T. Holmes III, 213-22. New York: Seabury,
1976.
"Formation and Transformation." In *Conversion: Perspectives
on Personal and Social Transformation*, ed. Walter E.
Conn, 23-26. New York: Alba House, 1978.

"Christian Theology of Human Rights." In *Understanding Human Rights*, ed. Alan D. Falconer, 224-36. Dublin: Irish School of Ecumenics, 1980.

"Is God Masculine?" In *Women in a Men's Church. Concilium* vol. 134, ed. Virgil Elizondo and Norbert Greinacher, 63-70. Edinburgh: T. & T. Clark, 1980.

"Afterword: Then and Now." In *Thomas Merton/Monk*, ed. Bro. Patrick Hart, 267-70. Kalamazoo, Mich.: Cistercian Publications; revised edition, 1983. Originally published in *Cistercian Studies* 13 (1978): 403-4.

"Spirituality for the Eighties." In *Christian Spirituality for the Eighties*, ed. Sandra J. Hirstein, 29-50. Dubuque, Iowa: William C. Brown, 1983.

"Liberating the Divine Energy." In *Living with Apocalypse: Spiritual Resources for Social Compassion*, ed. Tilden H. Edwards, 75-89. San Francisco: Harper & Row, 1984.

"Passionate Breakthrough – The Passionate God." In *Women's Spirituality*, ed. Joann Wolski Conn, 233-40. New York: Paulist, 1984.

"The Meaning of Marriage in Women's New Consciousness." In *Commitment to Partnership: Explorations of the Theology of Marriage*, ed. William P. Roberts, 141-57. New York: Paulist, 1987.

"Cultural Imperatives, Taboos, and the Gospel Alternative." In *The Vatican and Homosexuality*, eds. Jeannine Gramick and Pat Fuery, 201-207. New York: Crossroad, 1988.

"Belief and Culture." In *In All Things: Religious Faith and American Culture*, ed. Robert J. Daly, S.J., 156-78. Kansas City, Mo.: Sheed & Ward, 1990.

"The Fall of Babel: Reflections on the Abbey Center Conference." In *The Merton Annual,* vol. 6., ed. Michael Downey, George Kilcourse, Victor A. Kramer, 54-60. Collegeville: Liturgical Press, 1993.

"This I Believe: the Catholic Tradition." In *Reasoned Faith: Essays on the Interplay of Faith and Reason,* ed. Frank T. Birtel, 1-24. New York: Crossroad, 1993.

Articles in Periodicals

"Experience and Expression in Christian Education." *Life of the Spirit* 17 (1963): 533-38.

"The Parish House." *The Clergy Review* 48 (August 1963): 556-66.

"The Compassion of the Christ Child." *Marriage* 45:12 (December 1963): 12-17.

"Children and Sex." *Marriage* 46:3 (March 1964): 6-13.

"Home Church and Community." *Marriage* 46:10 (October 1964): 45-51.

"Autumn and Old Age." *Marriage* 46:11 (November 1964): 16-21.

"Teaching the Faith." *The Clergy Review* 50 (February 1965): 142-48.

"As God Sees Them." *Marriage* 47:3 (March 1965): 6-11.

"Christ's Law of Love." *Marriage* 48:1 (January 1966): 13-24.

"Education for a Journey: Some Ideas about Preparation for Marriage." *The Clergy Review* 51 (February 1966): 91-112.

"Don't Mistake Instruction for Religious Education." *Marriage* 48:2 (February 1966): 48-56.

"The Lesson of the Cross." *Marriage* 48:3 (March 1966): 47-56.

"The Risen Christ." *Marriage* 48:4 (April 1966): 54-62.

"The Kingdom of God." *Marriage* 48:5 (May 1966): 52-61.

"Life in Christ." *Marriage* 48:6 (June 1966): 16-22.

"What to Tell Children about Suffering." *Marriage* 48:7 (July 1966): 30-35.

"Freedom to Rethink Our Faith." *Marriage* 48:9 (September 1966): 12-18.

"The Weaker Sex." *The Clergy Review* 51 (November 1966): 849-62.

"The Radical Gap." *New Blackfriars* 48 (June 1967): 479-85.

"Faith or Works?" *The Catholic World* 205 (August 1967): 263-67.

"Open Experiments, Openly Arrived At." *Commonweal* 86 (25 August 1967): 511-13.

"Marriage and Virginity." *Doctrine and Life* 17 (November 1967): 587-96.

"The Church's Prophetic Vocation." *Sisters Today* 39 (January 1968): 211-29.

"People and Pigeon-Holes." *Doctrine and Life* 18 (January 1968): 3-8.

"The Ending of the Law." *Doctrine and Life* 18 (February 1968): 86-90.

"Abraham's Children." *Doctrine and Life* 18 (March 1968): 148-52.

"Teaching the Faith?" *Doctrine and Life* 18 (April 1968): 211-18.

"Spirituality." *Doctrine and Life* 18 (May 1968): 255-61.

"What Is a Family?" *Sign* 47:8 (May 1968): 15-19.

"Sex: The Hot Subject." *Doctrine and Life* 18 (June 1968): 333-39.

"The New Legalism." *Doctrine and Life* 18 (July 1968): 383-89.

"'We' and 'They' in the 1800's." *National Catholic Reporter* 4 (3 July 1968): 7.

"The Open Family." *Doctrine and Life* 18 (August 1968): 446-51.

"Anima Naturaliter Christiana." *Doctrine and Life* 18 (September 1968): 506-13.

"Conflict." *Doctrine and Life* 18 (October 1968): 577-81.

"Boredom." *Doctrine and Life* 18 (November 1968): 617-23.

"Experience of the New Church." *The Catholic World* 208 (November 1968): 5-6.

"The Uses of the Papacy." *The Catholic World* 208 (November 1968): 53-54.

"Either – Or." *The Catholic World* 208 (December 1968): 101-2.

"The Uses of the Papacy." *Doctrine and Life* 18 (December 1968): 693-700.

"What 'World'?" *The Catholic World* 208 (January 1969): 149-50.

"Moral Law." *The Catholic World* 208 (February 1969): 197-98.

"Truth or Compassion?" *The Catholic World* 208 (March 1969): 245-46.

"Children and the Good News." *Marriage* 51:4 (April 1969): 24-29.

"American Catholicism." *The Catholic World* 209 (April 1969): 5-6.

"Bridge Between Two Cultures." *The Catholic World* 209 (May 1969): 53-54.

"The Vision of Malines." *The Tablet* 223 (3 May 1969): 453.

"Too Much Money." *The Catholic World* 209 (June 1969): 101-2.

"Single Bliss." *The Catholic World* 209 (July 1969): 149-50.

"All Things in Common." *The Catholic World* 209 (August 1969): 197-98.

"Authority and Change." *Doctrine and Life* 19 (August 1969): 411-22.

"Christian Humanism." *The Catholic World* 209 (September 1969): 245-46.

"'As Little Children'?" *The Catholic World* 210 (October 1969): 5-6.

"And Who Is My Neighbor?" *The Catholic World* 210 (November 1969): 53-54.

"In Praise of Paul." *The Catholic World* 210 (December 1969): 101-2.

"Our God Is Not a Tame God." *The Catholic World* 210 (January 1970): 149-50.

"Marrying the Liturgy." *The Catholic World* 210 (February 1970): 197-98.

"Blueprint for a Family-Centered Community." *Marriage* 52:3 (March 1970): 56-61.

"Making Use of Middle Age." *The Catholic World* 210 (March 1970): 246-47.

"Christian and Pagan." *The Way* 10:2 (April 1970): 113-20.

"The Clerical Neurosis." *Doctrine and Life* 20 (April 1970): 175-84.

"Some Words on the Generation Gap." *The Catholic World* 211 (April 1970): 5-6.

"Clergy and People." *Doctrine and Life* 20 (May 1970): 268-76.

"It Would Have Been Different." *Marriage* 52:5 (May 1970) 57-61.

"Puritan's Ought and Paul's Ought." *The Catholic World* 211 (May 1970): 53-54.

"Back to the Woods." *The Catholic World* 211 (June 1970): 101-2.

"The Next Ten Years." *The Clergy Review* 55:6 (June 1970): 418-27.

"Present into Future." *Doctrine and Life* 20 (June 1970): 287-97.

"The Environment of Time." *The Catholic World* 211(July 1970): 149-50.

"Amid It All: Thanks." *Marriage* 52:8 (August 1970): 46-50.

"Let God Speak." *The Catholic World* 211 (August 1970): 197-98.

"Respectable or Christian?" *The Catholic World* 211 (September 1970): 245-46.

"An Educational Opportunity." *The Catholic World* 212 (October 1970): 7-8.

"The Routines of Life." *The Catholic World* 212 (November 1970): 63-64.

"Dawn of Reality." *The Catholic World* 212 (December 1970): 117-18.

"Bridges to the Past." *The Catholic World* 212 (January 1971): 175-76.

"Education for Wonder." *The Way* 11:1 (January 1971): 54-61.

"Sing to the Lord." *The Catholic World* 212 (February 1971): 230-31.

"The Art of Communication." *Marriage* 53:2 (February 1971): 67-71.

"Women's Lib." *The Catholic World* 212 (March 1971): 287-88.

"A Wedding and New Wine." *The Catholic World* 213 (May 1971): 62-63.

"Easing Our Burden." *The Catholic World* 213:1275 (June 1971): 119-20.

"No Substitutes." *The Catholic World* 213:1276 (July 1971): 167-68.

"Fairy Tales and a New Christian Awareness." *Doctrine and Life* 21 (August 1971): 395-403.

"Liturgical English." *The Catholic World* 213:1277 (August 1971): 215-16.

"Pretty Little Dresses, or Barefoot in Overalls?" *Marriage* 53:8 (August 1971): 56-61.

"The Braining of Maternity." *The Catholic World* 213:1278 (September 1971): 263-64.

"The Younger Son." *Doctrine and Life* 20 (September 1971): 465-473.

"Ambivalent Catholicism." *The Catholic World*, 214:1279 (October 1971): 7-8.

"'Cast Me Not Off in the Time of Old Age'." *Marriage* 53:11 (November 1971): 46-51.

"Judgment on the Earth." *The Catholic World* 214 (November 1971): 54-55.

"The Church as the Younger Son." *Doctrine and Life* 21 (December 1971): 663-673.

"The New Monasticism." *The Catholic World* 214:1281 (December 1971): 103-4.

"Self-Discovery: The Wisdom of the Animals." *Doctrine and Life* 22 (January 1972): 23-28.

"Sex Education and Religion." *New Catholic World* 215:1282 (January-February 1972): 12-13, 38-40.

"Waste Not, Want Not." *Marriage* 54:3 (March 1972): 24-29.

"Rediscovered Mission." *Sign* 51:7 (April 1972): 27.

"The Secret Earth." *Sign* 51:8 (May 1972): 19.

"Wanted Children." *Sign* 51:9 (June 1972): 11.

"One Thing Necessary." *Sign* 51:10 (July-August 1972): 17.

"Vision from the East." *Sign* 52:1 (September 1972): 21.

"What Children Are Really Like." *Marriage* 54:10 (October 1972): 32-37.

"Not By Bread Alone." *Sign* 52:2 (October 1972): 20.

"People Are Made for Joy." *Sign* 52:3 (November 1972): 39.

"New Adults Need Older Models." *Sign* 52:4 (December-January 1972-3): 20.

"A New World of Hope." *Sign* 52:5 (February 1973): 35.

"Why Should You Do Without?" *Sign* 52:6 (March 1973): 41.

"Echoes of the Gospel." *Sign* 52:7 (April 1973): 17.

"Conquering Domestic Stress." *Marriage* 55:5 (May 1973): 58-63.

"The Mother Who Hadn't the Knack." *Sign* 52:8 (May 1973): 23.

"The Uncivilized Culture." *Sign* 52:9 (June 1973): 35.

"Women for the Future." *Doctrine and Life* 23 (June 1973): 316-27.

"Unfulfilled Dreams and Dropping Out." *Sign* 52:10 (July-August 1973): 20.

"Discipline and Obedience." *Sign* 53:1 (September 1973): 25.

"Reflection – for What?" *Sign* 53:2 (October 1973): 19.

"Getting Out of It." *Sign* 53:3 (November 1973): 26.

"More 'Getting Out of It'." *Sign* 53:4 (December-January 1973-74): 19.

"Have They Lost Their Faith?" *Marriage* 56:2 (February 1974): 14-17.

"Lothlorien." *Sign* 53:5 (February 1974): 13.

"Shortage." *Sign* 53:7 (April 1974): 33.

"Young and Old(er)." *Sign* 53:8 (May 1974): 32.

"A Moral Tale." *Sign* 53:9 (June 1974): 19.

"Performing God's Play." *Sign* 53:10 (July/August 1974): 24.

". . . and go into the land which I will show you." *Doctrine and Life* 24 (August 1974): 431-40.

"Return of the Craftsman." *Sign* 54:1 (September 1974): 36.

"Spanking and Love." *Sign* 54:2 (October 1974): 15.

"Women in the Church." *The Way* 14:4 (October 1974): 288-95.

"Consider the Lilies." *Sign* 54:3 (November 1974): 18.

"Looking for Alternatives." *Sign* 54:4 (December-January 1974-5): 38.

"Books and Children." *Sign* 54:5 (February 1975): 21.

"'It's Always Winter –'." *Sign* 54:6 (March 1975): 17.

"A Crucial Question." *Sign* 54:7 (April 1975): 20.

"A British Eye's View." *Commonweal* 102:2 (11 April 1975): 41-43.

"'I Heard the Sound of Thee in the Garden'." *Sign* 54:8 (May 1975): 38.

"'. . . It Tolls for Thee'." *Sign* 54:9 (June 1975): 34.

"How Do You Celebrate?" *Sign* 54:10 (July-August 1975): 18.

"When to Be Different." *Sign* 55:1 (September 1975): 32.

"Understanding Death." *Sign* 55:2 (October 1975): 41.

"Stuck in One Place." *Sign* 55:3 (November 1975): 25.

"The Cardinal and Father John." *The Tablet* 229:7064 (22 November 1975): 1150-51.

"Our Rich Heritage." *Sign* 55:4 (December-January 1975-76): 25.

"On Being Relevant." *Sign* 55:5 (February 1976): 19.

"Family Spirituality: A Kind of Joy." *New Catholic World* 219:1310 (March-April 1976): 80-84.

"The Meat We Eat." *Sign* 55:7 (April 1976): 5.

"Five Women Who Shaped What We Believe." *Sign* 55:8 (May 1976): 18-23.

"Language Makes Us Human." *Sign* 55:8 (May 1976): 42.

"Authority in the Family." *Catholic Charismatic* 1:2 (May-June 1976): 8-11.

"Permanent Commitment." *Sign* 55:9 (June 1976): 15.

"Once Upon a Time Is Now." *Sign* 56:1 (September 1976): 9-11.

"The Impossible Enterprise." *Sign* 56:2 (October 1976): 24-27.

"Mary's Body Is Bread, Too." *Sign* 56:3 (November 1976): 28-33.

"Lothlorien: Where I Have to Be." *Sign* 56:5 (February 1977): 25-31.

"Women in the Church." *The Tablet* 231:7127 (12 February 1977): 149-50.

"Two Ways to Holiness." *Sign* 56:7 (April 1977): 20-27, 49.

"Three Women Who Dared." *Sign* 56:8 (May 1977): 18-27.

"Our Kind of Saints." *Sign* 56:9 (June 1977): 33-37.

"The Saints." *Catholic Charismatic* 2:2 (June-July 1977): 30-34.

"Something Important." *Sign* 57:5 (February 1978): 16-18.

"From Where I Stand." *The Tablet* 232:7188 (15 April 1978): 349-50.

"Updating the Church: Theology of Sexuality." *Doctrine and Life* 28 (June-July 1978): 324-39.

"A Catholic Understanding of Salvation." *Catholic Charismatic* 3:3 (September-October 1978): 4-8.

"The New Communities: A Challenge to the Church (1)." *Doctrine and Life* 29 (May 1979): 309-19.

"A Challenge to the Church: The New Communities (2)."
Doctrine and Life 29 (June-July 1979): 375-81.

"On Discovering Community." *Catholic Mind* 77:1334 (June 1979): 49-57.

"In Exchange with God." *National Catholic Reporter* 15 (1 June 1979): 1, 8.

"Sin, Like Redemption, Springs from the Body." *National Catholic Reporter* 15 (15 June 1979): 11.

"Bodily Symbolism." *National Catholic Reporter* 15 (29 June 1979): 16.

"Love Finds a Way." *National Catholic Reporter* 15 (13 July 1979): 24.

"God's Human Folly." *National Catholic Reporter* 15 (27 July 1979): 24.

"Born out of Weakness." *National Catholic Reporter* 15 (10 August 1979): 28.

"Comments on *Human Sexuality.*" *National Catholic Reporter* 15 (24 August 1979): 4, 20.

"A Challenge to the Church: The New Communities (3)." *Doctrine and Life* 29 (August-September 1979): 425-36.

"Good Enough for God." *Sign* 59:1 (September 1979): 37-40.

"The Evolving Language of Faith." *Sign* 61:4 (December-January 1981-2): 20-25.

"The Women Who Stayed." *Sign* 61:7 (April 1982): 36-41.

"We Caught the Touch of Incarnate Love." *National Catholic Reporter* 18 (8 October 1982): 15.

"The Emerging Church." *The Way* 23:1 (January 1983): 27-39.

"The Future Belongs to Those Who Have Been Pushed to a New Viewpoint." *National Catholic Reporter* 20 (2 March 1984): 15.

"Lent – No Time for Private Party." *National Catholic Reporter* 20 (9 March 1984): 13.

"Seeking New Forms of Community." *National Catholic Reporter* 20 (16 March 1984): 19.

"A Story of Healing Transformation." *National Catholic Reporter* 20 (23 March 1984): 16.

"Lent Means Transformation, Not Just 'Improvement'." *National Catholic Reporter* 20 (30 March 1984): 16.

"True Liturgy Touches Our Lives." *National Catholic Reporter* 20 (6 April 1984): 22.

"Easter: By Taking Risks We Become a New People." *National Catholic Reporter* 20 (13 April 1984): 14.

"The Economics of the Dispossessed." *Religion and Intellectual Life* 4 (Fall 1986): 23-33.

"The Friendship of God." *Pastoral Musician* 12 (October-November 1987): 29-35.

"The Language of Community." *Religion and Intellectual Life* 6 (Fall 1988): 112-17.

"Prophetic Spirituality." *Spiritual Life* 35:1 (Spring 1989): 3-12.

"Beyond Kith and Kin." *Marriage and Family* 71:8 (August 1989): 6-9.

"Prophecy in Exile." *Cross Currents* 39:4 (Winter 1989-90): 420-30.

"Your Family as Contemporary Prophets." *Marriage and Family* 72:2 (February 1990): 6-10.

"Does Commitment Mean Anything Anymore?" *Marriage and Family* 73:1 (January 1991): 10-13.

"Lent Can Be a Liberation for Women." *National Catholic Reporter* 27 (15 February 1991): 1, 24.

"Women Should Ponder before Rending Their Garments." *National Catholic Reporter* 27 (22 February 1991): 2.

"Dependence on God Found in Wilderness." *National Catholic Reporter* 27:18 (1 March 1991): 2.

"Liberation Isn't Just Changing the Bosses." *National Catholic Reporter* 27 (8 March 1991): 2.

"Patience and Passion Are Made for Each Other." *National Catholic Reporter* 27 (15 March 1991): 2.

"Jesus Knew Women as a Sex Suffer Most." *National Catholic Reporter* 27 (22 March 1991): 2.

"It Is Time for Women to Roll Away the Stone" *National Catholic Reporter* 27 (29 March 1991): 19.

"The Spirituality of Social Justice." *Sisters Today* 63:6 (November 1991): 402-14.

"Women and the Church." *Thought* 66 (December 1991): 398-412.

"Beyond Women's Ordination: The Church as Babel." With Nancy Schwoyer. *National Catholic Reporter* 30 (1 April 1994): 21.

"One Good Reason Why I'm Catholic." Essays by Rosemary Haughton et al. *U.S. Catholic* 59 (May 1994): 18-25.

"Open the Door." *U.S. Catholic* 59 (June 1994): 39-41

"Welfare Reform and National Scapegoating: The Politics of Fear." *Cross Currents* 45:1 (Spring 1995): 80-94.

"Personal Patrons: Three Lives That Shaped Mine." *U.S. Catholic* 60 (November 1995): 24-29.

Secondary Sources

Books

Abbott, Walter M., S.J. *The Documents of Vatican II.* New York: America Press, 1966.

Au, Wilkie, S.J. *By Way of the Heart: Toward a Holistic Christian Spirituality.* Mahwah, N.J.: Paulist, 1989.

Bacik, James J. *Spirituality in Transition.* Kansas City, Mo.: Sheed & Ward, 1996.

Baum, Gregory. *Religion and Alienation: A Theology of Human Experience.* New York: Paulist, 1978.

Birch, Charles, William Eakin, and Jay B. McDaniel, eds. *Liberating Life: Contemporary Approaches to Ecological Theology.* Maryknoll, N.Y.: Orbis Books, 1990.

Boff, Leonardo. *Ecclesiogenesis: The Base Communities Reinvent the Church.* Trans. Robert R. Barr. Maryknoll, N.Y.: Orbis Books, 1986.

Brown, Robert McAfee. *Spirituality and Liberation: Overcoming the Great Fallacy.* Philadelphia: Westminster, 1988.

Brueggemann, Walter. *The Prophetic Imagination.* Philadelphia: Fortress, 1978.

Buhlmann, Walter. *The Coming of the Third Church.* Slough, England: St. Paul Publications, 1974.

Callahan, Annice. *Spiritual Guides for Today.* New York: Crossroad, 1992.

Callahan, Annice, ed. *Spiritualities of the Heart: Approaches to Personal Wholeness in Christian Tradition.* New York: Paulist, 1990.

Campbell, Peter, and Edwin McMahon. *Bio-Spirituality.* Chicago: Loyola University Press, 1985.

Cantor, Norman F. *Twentieth Century Culture: Modernism to Deconstruction.* New York: Peter Lang Publishers, 1988.

Capra, Fritjof. *The Turning Point.* New York: Bantam Books, 1983.

Carmody, Denise Lardner. *Seizing the Apple: A Feminist Spirituality of Personal Growth.* New York: Crossroad, 1984.

_____. *Virtuous Woman: Reflections on Christian Feminist Ethics.* Maryknoll, N.Y.: Orbis Books, 1992.

Carmody, John. *Toward a Holistic Spirituality.* Mahwah, N.J.: Paulist, 1983.

Carr, Anne E. *A Search for Wisdom and Spirit: Thomas Merton's Theology of the Self.* Notre Dame: University of Notre Dame Press, 1988.

Carr, Anne E. *Transforming Grace: Christian Tradition and Women's Experience*. San Francisco: Harper & Row, 1988.

Condren, Mary. *The Serpent and the Goddess*. New York: Harper, 1989.

Conn, Joann Wolski. *Spirituality and Personal Maturity*. Mahwah, N.J.: Paulist, 1989.

Conn, Joann Wolski, ed. *Women's Spirituality: Resources for Christian Development*. New York: Paulist, 1986; Revised 2nd ed., 1996.

Conn, Walter E., ed. *Conversion: Perspectives on Personal and Social Transformation*. New York: Alba House, 1978.

Cunningham, Lawrence S., and Keith J. Egan. *Christian Spirituality: Themes from the Tradition*. Mahwah N.J.: Paulist, 1996.

Dictionnaire de spiritualité: ascétique et mystique doctrine et histoire. Vol. 14. Paris: Beauchesne, 1990.

Doohan, Leonard. *Laity's Mission in the Local Church*. San Francisco: Harper & Row, 1973.

Dorr, Donal. *Spirituality and Justice*. Maryknoll N.Y.: Orbis Books, 1984.

Downey, Michael., ed. *That They Might Live: Power, Empowerment, and Leadership in the Church*. New York: Crossroad, 1991.

Downey, Michael., ed. *The New Dictionary of Catholic Spirituality*. Collegeville: Liturgical Press, 1993.

Downey, Michael. *Understanding Christian Spirituality*. Mahwah, N.J.: Paulist, 1996.

Dreyer, Elizabeth A. *Earth Crammed with Heaven: A Spirituality of Everyday Life*. Mahwah N.J.: Paulist, 1994.

Dreyer, Elizabeth. *Manifestations of Grace*. Wilmington, Del.: Michael Glazier, 1990.

Dulles, Avery, S.J. *A Church to Believe In*. New York: Crossroad, 1983.

Dulles, Avery, S.J. *Models of the Church*. Garden City, N.Y.: Doubleday, 1974; expanded ed., 1987.

Dupré, Louis, and Donald Saliers, eds. *Christian Spirituality III: Post-Reformation and Modern*. World Spirituality: An Encyclopedic History of the Religious Quest, 18. New York: Crossroad, 1989.

Eigo, Francis, ed. *Contemporary Spirituality: Responding to the Divine Initiative*. Villanova: Villanova University Press, 1983.

_____. *Dimensions of Contemporary Spirituality*. Villanova: Villanova University, 1982.

Elizondo, Virgilio. *Christianity and Culture*. San Antonio: Mexican American Cultural Center, 1975.

Fabella, Virginia, Peter K. H. Lee, and David Kwang-sun Suh, eds. *Asian Christian Spirituality: Reclaiming Traditions*. Maryknoll, N.Y.: Orbis Books, 1992.

Fabella, Virginia, and Mercy Amba Oduyoye, eds. *With Passion and Compassion: Third World Women Doing Theology*. Maryknoll, N.Y.: Orbis Books, 1988.

Fischer, Kathleen. *Reclaiming the Connections: A Contemporary Spirituality*. Kansas City, Mo.: Sheed & Ward, 1990.

Fox, Mathew. *Original Blessing*. Santa Fe, N.M.: Bear and Company, 1987.

Garrigou-Lagrange, Reginald. *The Three Ages of the Interior Life*. 2 vols. Trans. T. Doyle. New York: Herder, 1948.

Graff, Ann O'Hara. *In the Embrace of God: Feminist Approaches to Theological Anthropology*. Maryknoll, N.Y.: Orbis Books, 1995.

Grey, Mary. *Feminism Redemption, and the Christian Tradition*. Mystic, Conn.: Twenty-Third Publications, 1990.

Griffin, David Ray, ed. *Spirituality and Society: Postmodern Visions*. New York: State University of New York, 1988.

Gutiérrez, Gustavo. *We Drink from Our Own Wells: The Spiritual Journey of a People.* Trans. Matthew J. O'Connell. New York: Orbis Books, 1984.

Haight, Roger, S.J. *An Alternative Vision: An Interpretation of Liberation Theology.* New York: Paulist, 1985.

Haight, Roger, S.J. *The Experience and Language of Grace.* New York: Paulist, 1979.

Hanson, Bradley C., ed. *Modern Christian Spirituality: Methodological and Historical Essays.* Atlanta: Scholars Press, 1990.

Holland, Joe. *Creative Communion: Toward a Spirituality of Work.* New York: Paulist, 1989.

Holland, Joe. *The Spiritual Crisis of Modern Culture.* Washington: Center of Concern, 1983.

Holland, Joe, and Peter Henriot. *Social Analysis: Communities, Social Action, and Theological Reflection.* New York: Paulist, 1983.

Holmes, Urban T. III. *Ministry and Imagination.* New York: Seabury, 1976.

Jaén, Néstor, S.J. *Toward a Liberation Spirituality.* Chicago: Loyola University Press, 1991.

Johnson, Elizabeth A. *Consider Jesus: Waves of Renewal in Christology.* New York: Crossroad, 1990.

Johnson, Elizabeth A. *She Who Is: The Mystery of God in Feminist Theological Discourse.* New York: Crossroad, 1993.

Jones, Cheslyn, Geoffrey Wainwright, and Edward Yarnold, eds. *The Study of Spirituality.* New York: Oxford University Press, 1986.

Kavanaugh, John Francis. *Following Christ in a Consumer Society: The Spirituality of Cultural Resistance.* Maryknoll, N.Y.: Orbis Books, 1986.

Kegan, Robert. *The Evolving Self: Problem and Process in Human Development.* Cambridge, Mass.: Harvard University Press, 1982.

Komonchak, Joseph A., Mary Collins, Dermot Lane, eds. *The New Dictionary of Theology*. Wilmington, Del.: Michael Glazier, 1987.

Lamb, Matthew. *Solidarity with Victims*. New York: Crossroad, 1982.

Lane, Dermot. *The Experience of God: An Invitation to Do Theology*. New York: Paulist, 1981.

Lane, Dermot. *Foundations for a Social Theology: Praxis, Process, and Salvation*. New York: Paulist, 1984.

Lonergan, Bernard J. F., S.J. *Method in Theology*. New York: Herder & Herder, 1973.

MacKinnon, Mary Heather and Moni McIntyre, eds. *Readings in Ecology and Feminist Theology*. Kansas City, Mo.: Sheed & Ward, 1995.

May, Rollo, ed. *Symbolism in Religion and Literature*. New York: Braziller, 1960.

McDaniel, Jay. *Earth, Sky, Gods and Mortals: Developing an Ecological Spirituality*. Mystic, Conn.: Twenty-Third, 1990.

McDermott, Brian O., S.J. *What Are They Saying About the Grace of Christ?* New York: Paulist, 1984.

McDonagh, Sean. *To Care for the Earth: A Call to a New Theology*. Santa Fe, N.M.: Bear and Company, 1987.

McFague, Sallie. *The Body of God: An Ecological Theology*. Minneapolis: Fortress, 1993.

McFague, Sallie. *Models of God: Theology for an Ecological, Nuclear Age*. Philadelphia: Fortress, 1987.

McFague, Sallie. *Speaking in Parables*. Philadelphia: Fortress, 1975.

McGinn, Bernard. *The Foundations of Mysticism*. Vol. 1, *The Presence of God: History of Western Christian Mysticism*. New York: Crossroad, 1991.

McGinn, Bernard, and John Meyendorff, eds. *Christian Spirituality I: Origins to the Twelfth Century*. World Spirituality: An Encyclopedic History of the Religious Quest, 16. New York: Crossroad, 1985.

Merton, Thomas. *The Asian Journal of Thomas Merton.* Naomi B. Stone et al., eds. New York: New Directions, 1973.

_____. *Conjectures of a Guilty Bystander.* New York: Doubleday and Co., 1966.

_____. *New Seeds of Contemplation.* New York: New Directions, 1972.

Miles, Margaret R. *Practicing Christianity: Critical Perspectives for an Embodied Spirituality.* New York: Crossroad, 1990.

Nouwen, Henri J. M. *Lifesigns.* New York: Doubleday, 1989.

O'Donovan, Leo J., ed. *A World of Grace.* New York: Crossroad, 1989.

Oliver, Mary Anne McPherson. *Conjugal Spirituality: The Primacy of Mutual Love in Christian Tradition.* Kansas City, Mo.: Sheed & Ward, 1996.

Overberg, Kenneth, S.J. *Roots and Branches: Grounding Religion in Human Experience.* Kansas City, Mo.: Sheed & Ward, 1991.

Pourrat, Pierre. *Christian Spirituality.* 4 vols. Trans. W. H. Mitchell and S. P. Jacques. Westminster, Md.: Newman, 1953-55.

Rahner, Karl, S.J. *The Shape of the Church to Come.* Trans. Edward Quinn. New York: Seabury, 1972.

_____. *Foundations of Christian Faith: An Introduction to the Idea of Christianity.* Trans. William V. Dych. New York: Seabury, 1978.

Rahner, Karl, and Herbert Vorgrimler, eds. *Dictionary of Theology.* New rev. ed. New York: Crossroad, 1985. S.v. "Experience," "Pastoral Theology."

Raitt, Jill, ed. *Christian Spirituality II: High Middle Ages and Reformation.* World Spirituality: An Encyclopedic History of the Religious Quest, 17. New York: Crossroad, 1987.

Richardson, A., and John Dowden, eds. *A New Dictionary of Christian Theology.* London: SCM Press, 1983.

Robinson, John A. T. *The Human Face of God.* London: SCM Press, 1973.

Ruether, Rosemary Radford. *Gaia and God: An Ecofeminist Theology of Earth Healing.* San Francisco: Harper, 1992.

_____. *Religion and Sexism: Images of Women in the Jewish and Christian Traditions.* New York: Simon & Schuster, 1974.

_____. *Sexism and God-talk.* Boston: Beacon, 1983.

_____. *Womanguides.* Boston: Beacon, 1985.

Schaef, Anne Wilson. *Women's Reality.* Minneapolis: Winston, 1981.

Schillebeeckx, Edward. *The Experience of Jesus as Lord.* New York: Crossroad, 1981.

Schüssler-Fiorenza, Elisabeth. *Bread Not Stone: The Challenge of Feminist Biblical Interpretation.* Boston: Beacon, 1984.

_____. *In Memory of Her: A Feminist Theological Reconstruction of Christian Origins.* New York: Crossroad, 1988.

Segundo, Juan Luis. *Grace and the Human Condition.* Maryknoll, N.Y.: Orbis Books, 1970.

Shea, John. *Stories of God.* Chicago: Thomas More, 1978.

Sheldrake, Philip. *Spirituality and History: Questions of Interpretation and Method.* New York: Crossroad, 1992.

Sobrino, Jon. *Christianity at the Crossroads.* Maryknoll, N.Y.: Orbis Books, 1978.

Soelle, Dorothee. *The Window of Vulnerability: A Political Spirituality.* Trans. Linda M. Maloney. Minneapolis: Fortress, 1990.

Stringfellow, William. *The Politics of Spirituality.* Philadelphia: Westminster, 1984.

Tanquerey, Adolphe. *The Spiritual Life: A Treatise on Ascetical and Mystical Theology.* 2nd ed. Tournai: Desclée, 1930.

Tinsley, Lucy. *The French Expressions for Spiritualité: A Semantic Study.* Washington, D.C.: Catholic University of America, 1953.

Toffler, Alvin. *Future Shock.* New York: Bantam Books, 1970.

_____. *Powershift: Knowledge, Wealth, and Violence at the Edge of the 21st. Century.* New York: Bantam Books, 1990.

_____. *The Third Wave.* New York: Bantam Books, 1980.

Tracy, David. *The Analogical Imagination: Christian Theology and the Culture of Pluralism.* New York: Crossroad, 1981.

_____. *Blessed Rage for Order: The New Pluralism in Theology.* New York: Seabury, 1975.

Wakefield, Gordon, ed. *Westminster Dictionary of Christian Spirituality.* Philadelphia: Westminster, 1983.

Weaver, Mary Jo. *New Catholic Women: A Contemporary Challenge to Traditional Religious Authority.* San Francisco: Harper & Row, 1985.

Welch, Sharon D. *Communities of Resistance and Solidarity: A Feminist Theology of Liberation.* Maryknoll, N.Y.: Orbis Books, 1985.

Whitehead, Evelyn Eaton, and James D. Whitehead. *A Sense of Sexuality: Christian Love and Intimacy.* New York: Doubleday, 1989.

_____. *The Emerging Laity: Returning Leadership to the Community of Faith.* New York: Doubleday, 1986.

_____. *The Promise of Partnership: Leadership and Ministry in an Adult Church.* San Francisco: Harper, 1991.

Woods, Richard, O.P. *Christian Spirituality: God's Presence through the Ages.* Chicago: Thomas More, 1989.

Woods, Richard, O.P., ed. *Understanding Mysticism*. Garden City, N.Y.: Image Books, 1980.

Young, Pamela Dickey. *Feminist Theology/Christian Theology*. Minneapolis: Augsburg Fortress, 1990.

Zappone, Katherine. *The Hope for Wholeness: A Spirituality for Feminists*. Mystic, Conn.: Twenty-Third Publications, 1991.

Articles in Periodicals

Alexander, Jon. "What Do Recent Writers Mean by Spirituality?" *Spirituality Today* 32 (1980): 246-56.

Baum, Gregory. "Faith and Culture." *The Ecumenist* 24:1(November/December 1985): 9-13.

Bechtle, Regina. "Convergences in Theology and Spirituality." *The Way* 23 (1985): 305-14.

_____. "Reclaiming the Truth of Women's Lives: Women and Spirituality." *The Way* 28 (1988): 50-58.

Boff, Leonardo. "Theological Characteristics of a Grassroots Church." In *The Challenge of Basic Christian Communities*, ed. Sergio Torres and John Eagleson. Maryknoll N.Y.: Orbis Books, 1982, 124-44.

Brennan, Margaret. "'In the End the Lion is God': A Reflection on the Sacred in Experience." *The Way* 28 (1988): 5-18.

Britten, Kathlene. "Rosemary Haughton at Home." *Way-Catholic Viewpoint* 26:3 (April 1970): 26-34.

Callahan, Annice, R.S.C.J. "The Relationship between Spirituality and Theology." *Horizons* 16 (1989): 266-74.

Callahan, William R., S.J. "Spirituality and Justice: An Evolving Vision of the Great Commandment." In *Contemporary Spirituality*, ed. Francis A. Eigo, O.S.A., 137-61. Villanova: Villanova University Press, 1983.

Carr, Anne E. "Starting with the Human." In *A World of Grace*, ed. Leo O'Donovan, 17-30. New York: Crossroad, 1989.

_____. "Theology and Experience in the Thought of Karl Rahner." *The Journal of Religion* 53 (1973): 359-76.

Cenker, William. "Theme and Counter-Theme in Contemporary Spirituality." *Horizons* 9:1 (Spring 1982): 87-95.

Christ, Carol P. "Embodied Thinking." *Journal of Feminist Studies in Religion* 5:1 (Spring 1989): 7-15.

Clarke, Thomas E., S.J. "A New Way: Reflecting on Experience." In *Tracing the Spirit: Communities, Social Action, and Theological Reflection*, ed. James E. Hug, S.J., 13-37. New York: Paulist, 1983.

Collins, Sheila D. "The Personal Is Political." In *The Politics of Women's Spirituality*, ed. Charlene Spretnak, 362-67. New York: Doubleday, 1982.

Conn, Joann Wolski, et al. "Review Symposium." Review of *The Passionate God*, by Rosemary Haughton. *Horizons* 10 (Spring 1983): 124-40.

Conn, Joann Wolski. "Horizons on Contemporary Spirituality." *Horizons* 9:1 (1982): 60-73.

Conn, Walter E. "Affective Conversion: The Transformation of Desire." In *Religion and Culture*, ed. Timothy P. Fallon, S.J., and Philip Riley, 261-76. Albany: State University of New York, 1987.

Cousins, Ewert H. "Spirituality: A Resource for Theology." *Catholic Theological Society of America Proceedings* 35 (1980): 124-37.

Crysdale, Cynthia. "Development, Conversion, and Religious Education." *Horizons* 17, no. 1 (1990): 30-46.

Cunningham, Lawrence S. "Sages, Wisdom, and the Catholic Tradition." Warren Lecture Series. Tulsa: University of Tulsa Press, 1993.

Derrick, Christopher. Review of *Transformation of Man* by Rosemary Haughton. *Tablet* 221, 12 August 1967, 864.

Doohan, Helen. "Today's Church Needs Women's Leadership." *Human Development* 7:2 (Summer 1986): 7-11.

Doohan, Leonard. "Lay People and the Church." *The Way* 32 (1992): 168-77.

Downey, Michael. "Understanding Christian Spirituality: Dress Rehearsal for a Method." *Spirituality Today* 43 (Fall 1991): 271-80.

Dreyer, Elizabeth. "Tradition and Lay Spirituality: Problems and Possibilities." *Spirituality Today* 39 (1987): 196-210.

Dulles, Avery, S.J. "The Meaning of Faith Considered in Relationship to Justice." In *The Faith that Does Justice*, ed. John C. Haughey, 10-46. New York: Paulist, 1977.

Dupré, Louis. "Spirituality Confronts the Modern World." *Communio* 12 (Spring 1985): 334-41.

Elias, John L. "The Return of Spirituality: Contrasting Interpretation." *Religious Education* 86 (Summer 1991): 455-65.

Gallagher, Michael Paul. Review of *The Passionate God* by Rosemary Haughton. *The Furrow* 32 (November 1981): 757-78.

Garafalo, Rob. "Through a Glass Darkly: Spirituality and Ecclesiology after the Council." *Spiritual Life* 38:1 (1992): 13-24.

Gutiérrez, Gustavo. "Drink from Your Own Well." In *Learning to Pray. Concilium* 159, ed. C. Floristán and C. Duquoc, 38-45. New York: Seabury, 1982.

Halkes, Catherina. "Feminism and Spirituality." *Spirituality Today* 40 (1988): 220-36.

Hamm, Dennis. Review of *The Transformation of Man* by Rosemary Haughton. In *America* 117 (2 December 1967): 692-93.

Heagle, John. "A New Public Piety – Reflections on Spirituality." *Church* 1:3 (Fall 1985): 52-55.

Holland, Joe. "Beyond a Privatized Spirituality." *New Catholic World* 231 (July/August 1988): 175-78.

Holland, Joe. "Linking Social Analysis and Theological Reflection: The Place of Root Metaphors in Social and

Religious Experience." In *Tracing the Spirit: Communities, Social Action, and Theological Reflection,* ed. James E. Hug, S.J., 170-91. New York: Paulist, 1983.

Holland, Joseph. "The Post-Modern Paradigm Implicit in the Church's Shift to the Left." In *Faith That Transforms,* ed. Mary Jo Leddy and Mary Ann Hinsdale, 39-61. New York: Paulist, 1987.

Howie, Maureen. Review of *The Passionate God* by Rosemary Haughton. *Heythrop Journal* 24 (April 1983): 221-22.

Imbelli, Robert. Review of *The Passionate God* by Rosemary Haughton. *Commonweal* 10 (25 February 1983): 119-20.

Jones, Arthur. "Laity Climbs Circular Stairs to Church Empowerment." *National Catholic Reporter,* 13 October 1989, 5.

Jones, Arthur. "One Woman's Progress." *Tablet* 238 (28 January 1984): 79-80.

Kinast, Robert L. "How Pastoral Theology Functions." *Theology Today* 37 (January 1981): 425-39.

_____. "Theological Reflection in Ministry Preparation." In *Tracing the Spirit: Communities, Social Action, and Theological Reflection,* ed. James E. Hug, S.J. New York: Paulist, 1983, 83-99.

King, J. Norman. "The Experience of God in the Theology of Karl Rahner." *Thought* 53 (1978): 174-201.

Laguë, M. "Spiritualité et théologie: d'une même souche: Notes sur l'actualité d'un debat." *Église et théologie* 20 (1989): 333-351.

Lamb, Matthew. "Christian Spirituality and Social Justice." *Horizons* 10 (1983): 32-49.

_____. "The Theory-Praxis Relationship in Contemporary Christian Theologies." *Catholic Theological Society of America Proceedings* 31 (1976): 149-78.

Lambert, Pierrot, Charlotte Tansey, and Cathleen Going, eds. *Caring about Meaning: Patterns in the Life of Bernard Lonergan.* Montreal: Thomas More Institute, 1982.

Leclerq, Jean. "'Spiritualitas.'" *Studi medievali* 3 (1962): 279-96.

Leonard, Ellen. "Experience as a Source for Theology: A Canadian and Feminist Perspective." *Studies in Religion/Sciences religieuses* 19 (Spring 1990): 143-62.

Lilburn, Tim, S.J. "Rosemary Haughton's Hope." *Sisters Today* 53 (May 1982): 515-19.

Loewe, William P. Review of *The Passionate God* by Rosemary Haughton. *Commonweal* 109 (17 December 1982): 695.

Lonergan, Bernard, S.J. "Theology and Praxis." *Catholic Theological Society of America Proceedings* 32 (1977): 1-16.

Lonergan Research Institute Bulletin, Spring 1977. Lonergan Research Institute, Toronto.

McCann, Dennis P. "The Passionate God." Review of *On Trying to Be Human, The Transformation of Man, The Theology of Experience, The Catholic Thing,* and *The Passionate God* by Rosemary Haughton. In *Anglican Theological Review* 65 (April 1983): 206-13.

McFague, Sallie. "Conversion: Life on the Edge of the Raft." *Interpretation* 32 (1978): 255-68.

Murphy, Ann Rita. Review of *Song in a Strange Land,* by Rosemary Haughton. *Sisters Today* 63 (May 1991): 220.

"New Shoots? An Interview with Rosemary Haughton" (Saskatoon, 1984). *Canadian Catholic Review* 3, no. 1 (January 1985): 4.

O'Collins, Gerald. "Theology and Experience." *Irish Theological Quarterly* 44 (1977): 279-90.

O'Donoghue, Noel D. Review of *The Passionate God,* by Rosemary Haughton. *Irish Theological Quarterly* 49, no. 3 (1982): 216-17.

O'Donovan, Leo J., S.J., ed. "A Changing Ecclesiology in a Changing Church: A Symposium on Development in the Ecclesiology of Karl Rahner." *Theological Studies* 38 (1977): 736-62.

Ohanneson, J. "Author Rosemary Haughton Moves Her Brood to Remote Site in Scotland." *National Catholic Reporter* 10 (10 May 1974): 4-5.

Osiek, Carolyn, R.S.C.J. "Reflections on an American Spirituality." *Spiritual Life* 22 (1976): 230-40.

Parrella, Frederick J. "Spirituality in Crisis: The Search for Transcendence in our Therapeutic Culture." *Spirituality Today* 35 (1983): 292-303.

Pasquier, Jacques. "Experience and Conversion." *The Way* 17 (1977): 114-22.

Patrick, Anne E. "Ethics and Spirituality: The Social Justice Connection." *The Way Supplement* 63 (Autumn 1988): 103-16.

Principe, Walter. "Pluralism in Christian Spirituality." *The Way* 32:1 (January 1992): 54-61.

Principe, Walter. "Toward Defining Spirituality." *Studies in Religion/Sciences religieuses* 12 (1983): 127-41.

Purvis, Sally B. "Christian Feminist Spirituality." In *Christian Spirituality III: Post-Reformation and Modern*, eds. Louis Dupré and Don E. Salier, 500-19. World Spirituality: An Encyclopedic History of the Religious Quest, 18. New York: Crossroad, 1989.

Rahner, Karl. "Basic Theological Interpretation of the Second Vatican Council." *Theological Investigations* 20, 77-89. Trans. Edward Quinn. New York: Crossroad, 1981.

_____. "Courage for an Ecclesial Church." *Theological Investigations* 20, 3-12. Trans. Edward Quinn. New York: Crossroad, 1981.

_____. "The Church of Sinners." *Theological Investigations* 6, 253-69. Trans. Karl-Heinz and Boniface Kruger. London: Darton, Longman and Todd, 1969.

_____. "The Development of Dogma." *Theological Investigations* 1, 39-78. Trans. Cornelius Ernst. London: Darton, Longman and Todd, 1961.

_____. "The Function of the Church as a Critic of Society." *Theological Investigations* 12, 229-49. Trans. David Bourke. New York: Seabury, 1974.

_____. "Reflections on the Experience of Grace." *Theological Investigations* 3, 86-90. Trans. Karl-H. and Boniface Kruger. New York: Seabury, 1967.

_____. "The Spirituality of the Future." In *The Practice of Faith: A Handbook of Contemporary Spirituality,* ed. K. Lehmann and A. Raffelt, 18-26. New York: Crossroad, 1986.

_____. "The Spirituality of the Church of the Future." *Theological Investigations* 20, 143-53. Trans. Edward Quinn. New York: Crossroad, 1981.

Risley, John. "Liberation Spirituality." *Spirituality Today* 35 (1983): 127-40.

Robb, Paul V., S.J. "Conversion as a Human Experience." *Studies in the Spirituality of Jesuits* 14 (May 1982): 1-50.

Ruether, Rosemary Radford. "Crises and Challenges of Catholicism Today," *America* 154 (1 March 1986): 152-58.

_____. "Theologizing from the Side of the Other." In *Faith that Transforms,* ed. Mary Jo Leddy and Mary Ann Hinsdale, 62-81. New York: Paulist, 1987.

Schneiders, Sandra M. "Effects of Women's Experience on Spirituality." In *Women's Spirituality: Resources for Christian Development,* ed. Joann Wolski Conn. New York: Paulist, 1986.

_____. "Spirituality in the Academy." *Theological Studies* 50 (1989): 676-97.

Schneiders, Sandra M., I.H.M. "Theology and Spirituality: Strangers, Rivals or Partners?" *Horizons* 13 (1986): 253-74.

_____. "Scripture and Spirituality." In *Christian Spirituality I: Origins to the Twelfth Century*, Bernard McGinn and John Meyendorff, eds., 1-20. World Spirituality: An Encyclopedic History of the Religious Quest 16. New York: Crossroad, 1985.

Shea, John. "Introduction: Experience and Symbol: An Approach to Theologizing." *Chicago Studies* 19 (1980): 5-20.

Smith, Marion. Review of *The Passionate God,* by Rosemary Haughton. In *The Month* 14 (October 1981): 356.

Sucocki, Marjorie Hewitt. "Earthsong, Godsong: Women's Spirituality." *Theology Today* 45 (1988): 392-400.

TeSelle, Sallie. Review of *Tales from Eternity,* by Rosemary Haughton. In *Commonweal* 100 (5 April 1974): 114-16.

Tetlow, Joseph, S.J. "Spirituality. An American Sampler." *America* 153 (1985): 261-67.

Tucker, Mary Evelyn. "New Perspectives for Spirituality." *Religion and Intellectual Life* 6:2 (Winter 1989): 48-56.

Vacek, Edward, S.J. "Development within Rahner's Theology." *The Irish Theological Quarterly* 42 (1975): 36-49.

Wilson, Anne. "Holistic Spirituality." *Spirituality Today* 40 (Autumn 1988): 208-19.

Zappone, Katherine. "Feminist Spirituality and the Transformation of Religious Experience." *Studies* 76 (1987): 60-68.

Index

Some Haughton modifiers will be found under the name Rosemary Haughton; others are listed under more specific headings.